How to Eat with One Hand

How to Eat with One Hand

Recipes and Other Nourishment for New and Expectant Parents

Christine Flynn
and
Emma Knight

b80119

手抓饭 – 第1次印刷

PENGUIN

an imprint of Penguin Canada, a division of Penguin Random House Canada Limited

Canada • USA • UK • Ireland • Australia • New Zealand • India • South Africa • China

First published 2021

www.penguinrandomhouse.ca

Library and Archives Canada Cataloguing in Publication

Title: How to eat with one hand : recipes and other nourishment for new and
    expectant parents / Christine Flynn and Emma Knight.
Names: Flynn, Christine, 1983- author. | Knight, Emma (Emma L.), author.
Identifiers: Canadiana (print) 20200238736 | Canadiana (ebook) 20200238744 |
    ISBN 9780735239999 (softcover) | ISBN 9780735240001 (EPUB)
Subjects: LCSH: Make-ahead cooking. | LCSH: Motherhood. | LCGFT: Cookbooks.
Classification: LCC TX652 .F59 2020 | DDC 641.5/55—dc23

Cover and book design by Leah Springate
Cover and interior photography by Suech and Beck
Food and prop styling by Emily Howes

Printed and bound in China

10 9 8 7 6 5 4 3 2 1

For Piper, Matilda, Esmé and Frida

CONTENTS

Cravings

The part when you're pregnant and revelling in highly specific food hankerings.

The Big Chill

The part when birth is imminent and you're preparing yourself, mind, body and freezer.

One Hand, One Love

The part when you're hungrier than ever and always holding a baby (at least one).

A Full Plate

The part when your baby (and then, suddenly, toddler) has joined the family table.

Home Economics

The part when you're creating a world for your children.

Building Blocks

Stocks, sauces, spreads and one dough.

INTRODUCTION

[Emma] We wrote this for the expectant mother who hasn't yet told anyone at work and is mouth-breathing through the nausea, trying hard not to fall asleep standing up. And for the new parent on their hands and knees in a pitch-black bedroom with a screaming baby slung over their shoulder, patting the floor to find a pacifier that is made of rubber, so it could have bounced f*cking anywhere.

This book is written by, but not exclusively for, mothers. Motherhood takes many forms, and any front-line parent or caregiver is likely to need a great deal of sustenance, both edible and emotional. And so, to our fellow new mom-and-dad-types, we offer this collection of simple, comforting recipes for each stage of early parenthood—to be devoured with the one baby-free hand at your disposal—plus a glimpse behind the blackout curtain of new motherhood as we are experiencing it.

[Christine] I didn't fully respect what it meant to be a mother until I became one. Twice. In fact, if anyone ever considered me blasé about anything, it would have been pregnancy. But then there was the seven-minute span when I first held one baby in my arms, and then another. It was like that scene in *The Wizard of Oz* where everything goes from black and white to colour. My world exploded with every feeling and emotion, and I was turned inside out and left, quite literally, empty and waiting for things to shift back into place. Becoming a mom has been both harder and more wonderful than anything I could have imagined.

It is also intensely lonely. There's a "grin and bear it" mentality to which many of us default. We aren't the first women to find ourselves uncomfortably pregnant or willing a snuffling infant to latch (but gently!) or, as I am now, constantly arguing with toddlers. Of course we aren't the first, but it's the first time for us. Unprepared as I was, I found myself compelled to offer other pregnant women support—"Do you need anything?" "How are you doing?" "I made 32 gallons of soup, would you like some?!"—and tried my best to be an open book about what had worked (or not) for me. Candour is the best gift you can give an expectant mother. That, and maybe an Eggplant Parmesan (page 50). While much of this book was written with our thumbs, Emma and I had an unwavering vision of what it should and could be.

[E] You know that feeling when you're at a sink in a public washroom, holding your hands under an automatic tap that won't turn on? You try going closer to the faucet, further from the faucet, waving your hands in front of the sensor and under neighbouring taps—to no avail. Maybe someone a few taps down is washing her hands successfully as if there's nothing to it. A lot of early motherhood can feel like that.

But then sometimes someone appears at your shoulder and holds her hand under your tap in exactly the right place in a non-smug, *it's not you, these taps are impossible* kind of way. We want this book to be that person. Because those taps are not always automatic, and neither is motherhood. There are many sweet spots, but we need to help each other find them.

No two experiences of motherhood are alike, and certainly Christine's and mine have been very different. But she was in many ways that person for me.

The idea for this book came about over text messages around dinnertime. Christine had just told me that Spanish Tortilla (page 208) is "great mom food," by which she meant simple, delicious, inexpensive, one-handable and easily gummed by curious onlookers. An idea lodged itself in my brain and caused me to burn myself while browning zucchini.

"What about a collection of recipes, plus essays about what it's really like?" I asked, attaching an image of my singed wrist.

"I think you might be half-serious, and I am too," Christine replied.

Later that same night, as we sent recipe and essay ideas back and forth until 2 AM, she supplied a title, in homage to M.F.K. Fisher's *How to Cook a Wolf,* which is also about living and eating well under difficult circumstances: *How to Eat with One Hand.*

WHAT TO EXPECT (FROM THIS BOOK)

[E] With this book, we hope to offer a path to meaningful nourishment as well as adult company and reassurance that the baby will, eventually, fall asleep so you can eat your darned sandwich.

The way we've organized the recipes is somewhat atypical: instead of meal occasion or time of day, they're classified by phase of motherhood. In the first chapter, Cravings, there are recipes that fit the unique food needs of pregnancy—but are equally delicious for the non-pregnant among us. The second chapter, The Big Chill, is made up of recipes to batch cook and stockpile in your freezer while you still can. The third chapter, One Hand, One Love, is filled with nutritious things to devour in your PJs during the ravenous first few months postpartum. The fourth, A Full Plate, is dedicated to comforting family meals beloved by adults and young eaters alike that will help make the transition from baby to toddler less stressful and more delicious for all involved. In the fifth chapter, Home Economics, we've shared the DIYs that have kept us (mostly) afloat through the whitewater rapids of new parenthood.

We hope this won't stop you from making any of these recipes whenever you please. The phases addressed in our chapters are fleeting (too fleeting, as strangers might feel the need to remind you, peering first into your stroller and then into your soul), but if we've done our job well, these recipes should go on being useful well beyond the finish line of "early" parenthood, wherever that is located.

In between recipes, we've included first-person essays written from within the various phases of early motherhood. With these essays, we've tried to capture a period of rapid change and intense emotion that's impossible to imagine beforehand and difficult to conjure in any detail after the fact. Our wild wish is that even one reader might, at some point in these pages, laugh darkly and know she's not alone.

YOU CAN GO YOUR OWN WAY

[C] Cooking is a science, but it's not an *exact* science. In writing this book, Emma and I tried as best we could to use vegetables as units (1 carrot versus ½ cup/125 mL carrot) because it makes shopping easier, and there is nothing more annoying than having to wrap up three-quarters of a yellow onion and put it back in the fridge. If your onions or potatoes or what have you are a bit bigger or a bit smaller than ours, none of these recipes will look dramatically different.

The recipes *will* look dramatically different if you don't follow the instructions, however. Working in restaurants for twenty years, I've noticed that most mistakes happen when people read the ingredients list and not the actual recipe. So, go ahead and read the recipe before you start. Then read it again and visualize each step. I know, I know, I sound a bit woo-woo here, but I'm not advising you to do this just so you can cook mindfully and with intent (though that is nice), but also so that you are more likely to have everything you need (including equipment!) and less likely to make a mistake—which often slows you down a lot more than scanning a recipe once or twice before you crack on.

In terms of substitutions and tweaks, go for it. Things like garnishes can often simply be removed (Don't like cilantro on your Chilaquiles, page 179? Just leave it off!), and we would never tell you *not* to add hot sauce or some wilted greens to a recipe that might benefit (Mulligatawny, page 192! Red Flannel Hash, page 119!). For larger modifications that fundamentally change the recipe, again, we say go for it but with the caveat that you try it our way first, so you know the techniques and flavour profile you're aiming for.

We want you to use this book. We want you to scribble notes in the margins and dog-ear pages with recipes that look delicious or comforting or useful to you. We want you to cook for yourself and ask other people to cook for you using this book, because you deserve delicious, thoughtful food all the time—but right now, especially. We've given you a list of what might not be considered classics, but they are *our* classics. We hope these recipes will make it into regular rotation (with a bit of your own flair) in your home as well.

THE PREGNANT PANTRY

[C] People were surprised when I became pregnant (so was I, but for different reasons). One of my cousins emailed me, and right smack in the middle of it she wrote, "It's difficult to picture you as a mother." Among the many thoughts I had was the overwhelming sense that, actually, I had better training than most. I'm a cook, after all—used to long hours, difficult working conditions and questionable management. I had no illusions about what motherhood would be like and knew that all I could do was be prepared and hang on.

Cooking teaches you all about the concept of *mise en place*, or "everything in its place." It means having what you need, knowing where it is and refilling before you run out. For the day, for the week, for the next nine months and beyond. It's useful as a household strategy in general, but once you're responsible for a human other than yourself, it becomes a requirement. Not for the other human per se (although they do benefit), but so that you can sidestep the pitfalls that occur when you don't have your shit together. When you have mise en place, you can stay calm when things go sideways. Or, *reasonably* calm.

Mise en place can mean making your bed each day, or always having six frozen bags of breast milk in your freezer. What makes you feel "mised" is very personal. It does, however, start in the kitchen, and I've compiled a desert island list for you. It's longer than your typical cookbook pantry list, because we understand that there are times when you might not be able to get outside for a few days or longer and because we prize variety almost as much as we prize organization. It's also broken up into sections, a further nod to keeping everything in its place.

DRY GOODS

Salt

Kosher salt is our salt of choice. It has enough texture to it that you can feel how much you're adding, and we like to keep a small dish next to the stove for seasoning as we go. For finishing a dish, use a flakey sea salt like Maldon or Annapolis Salt Company.

Pepper

I have a long and tortured history with black pepper, because I lived through the 90s when steak au poivre was a thing and you'd have to crunch through entire black peppercorns to get to the meat, often while a waiter hovered nearby with a comically large pepper grinder, ready to supply auxiliary pepper should you require more. As a result, I'm selective about where I put my pepper and am adamant about a fine grind. Whole peppercorns are the only choice. Get yourself a grinder and don't even bother with the pre-ground stuff, as all the good flavour is lost already.

Olive Oil

If it's in your budget, have one "daily use" olive oil for cooking, baking, poaching, what have you and then a better-quality one for finishing salads, drizzling over cheese or roasted vegetables and so on. A high-quality oil will be slightly bitter with a spicy aftertaste.

Vinegar

Vinegar is essential for when you need that hit of acid, and fresh citrus isn't available or simply isn't strong enough. Most people have a preferred vinegar, which tends to have a lot to do with whatever dusty bottle was in their family's cupboard growing up. I love raw apple cider vinegar. It's tart enough to finish a sturdy salad but has enough sweetness that I'll use it in baking. Recently, I've taken to plain old white vinegar, which is great for adding a very clean acidic flavour to salads and stews, and also for general cleaning around the house. Rice wine vinegar and a good balsamic vinegar are also handy to have around. Don't be afraid to use a few different vinegars in a single dish; it's a great way to add depth of flavour.

Beans

Dried and canned. There's something homey and wonderful about having a pot of beans bubbling on the stove, but when in a hurry there's no shame in reaching for some canned beans. Favourites to have on hand are chickpeas, black beans and white navy beans.

Canned Tomatoes

In our kitchens, tomatoes are a heavy lifter. Pizza sauce, pasta sauce, stews, rice, curries— you name it, we've put a can of tomatoes in it. San Marzano tomatoes are best for quality and flavour. We prefer whole tomatoes, but go ahead and buy crushed or diced if that's what you like.

Grains

Grains that you can cook quickly are a must. Rice, pasta and polenta are all simple to prepare and filling. Choose the best quality you can afford and purchase small-ish quantities. Even though they're a dry good, they can go stale, so use the older grains first and continue to replenish your pantry with a fresh supply as needed.

All-Purpose Flour, Granulated Sugar, Baking Powder, Baking Soda

This is your basic baking starter pack. Regardless of how fluent you are (or are not) with the ins and outs of baking, we like to think this book will inspire you (yes, you!) to roll up your sleeves and get outside your comfort zone with some comfort cookery. Muffins, scones, breads, pancakes—they're all in here, and the first step is just to have the ingredients on hand.

Coconut Milk

Coconut milk is perfect for finishing curries, especially if you need to temper the spice level for a junior spice threshold. It's also a great dairy alternative for things like chia pudding and can be used as a simple topping for fresh fruit. We use full-fat coconut milk and always have at least two cans buried in the back of our cupboards for emergencies.

Spices

I get overwhelmed whenever I open a spice cupboard and there are bags exploding, unlabelled jars teetering and at least three boxes of cornstarch. I keep a fairly slim selection, and you generally can get pretty far with paprika, caraway seeds, cumin seeds, za'atar (technically a blend!), fennel seeds and ground cinnamon. Spices have a shelf life, so it's important to cull the herd every once in a while and toss anything that tastes stale.

FRIDGE

Butter

Unsalted butter is the only butter that exists in my world. Use the basic stuff for cooking and baking, splurge occasionally on the cultured stuff for an excellent cinnamon toast or to pair with warm Sour Cream Scones (page 97). You deserve it.

Citrus Fruits

Always fresh, always lots. Thinly slice whole lemons and add them to creamy, crisp salads for acid and a touch of bitterness. Squeeze limes over a spicy dish to make it hum with flavour. Keep grapefruits ice cold in the fridge and serve the segments alongside thinly sliced fennel or swimming in their own juice for a quick breakfast. If you can't afford fresh citrus, or you can't get to the grocery store, go back and check out the Vinegar section (page 8)!

Herbs

Chopped, torn, minced, smashed, whole—herbs add a little of what the French call, "I don't know what" to your dishes. Buy them by the bunch or grow them on your windowsill, and if things start to look tired, freeze any extra to add to stews, soups, sauces or dressings later on. We like all herbs, but our top three are basil, cilantro and flat-leaf parsley (known affectionately by chefs as "FLP"), because they are the most versatile—and also because you can finely chop the stems and use those too.

Cheese

A hard cheese that lasts forever, such as Pecorino or an aged Gouda, is handy for grating over things (cheese snow!) or serving with a glass of ice-cold Chablis. A softer (cheaper) cheese, such as mozzarella or white cheddar, is good for melting onto cheese toast, finishing a pizza or slicing for a snack.

Sour Cream

You can always swap out Greek yogurt for sour cream, but we like the balance between sour and creamy that sour cream offers, as opposed to skewing toward the "tangy" flavour of yogurt. Whatever your thick dairy preference, go for full-fat and dollop it generously on soups, stews, hashes and fry-ups, or use it in baked goods.

Eggs

Eggs are a cheap, quick and simple meal. If you can find a local source where the chickens are well fed and cared for, you'll notice a big difference in flavour and texture.

Pickles

Everyone has a favourite pickle—make sure yours is always in the fridge. A cold, crunchy pickle is a great foil for spicy or fatty dishes, and you can even use the pickle brine in a salad dressing or to make a Big Mac–style aioli to spread on sandwiches and other bready situations.

Mustard

Again, a very personal decision. I often have a large quantity of yellow mustard on hand and a small quantity of tarragon Dijon, whereas Emma prefers the more classic Maille Dijon Originale. Whatever your preference, with mustard on hand you will be able to whip up a delicious vinaigrette or elevate the taste of a simple sandwich with one quick slather.

Hot Sauce

I'm a Cholula girl myself, but I've been known to dabble with Valentina, Sriracha or even Frank's RedHot. Whatever your hot sauce preference, make sure it's one you like as much on tacos as on eggs. You need a multitasker, not eighteen different mini bottles taking up precious fridge real estate.

Nut or Seed Butter

Spread it on toast, thicken salad dressings, whip up a smoothie or make hummus with a good nut or seed butter. These are often pricey, but if you use them judiciously, they go a long way. Ready-made cashew, almond and sesame seed butters are all favourites to have on hand, but we also give you a recipe for Cinnamon Pecan Butter (page 257) so you can make your own.

FREEZER

Fruit

Buy organic frozen fruit in bulk. It's more economical, and it's convenient. It's also difficult to rationalize spending a fortune on fresh fruit when at this point in our parenting journeys, at least half of it is going to get hurled to the floor. Blueberries, cherries and raspberries are household favourites, for eating straight from the freezer, blitzing into smoothies and folding into pancakes, muffins and scones.

Cheese Rinds

Save the rinds from hard cheeses like Parmesan or Pecorino and freeze them. Slipping one or two into a brothy saucepan of beans or a long-simmering pasta sauce adds richer flavour and can soften sharp flavours like lemon or tomatoes. Simply remove the rinds before serving. You can also give frozen rinds to your kids to gnaw on when they are teething—they work like a charm!

Yeast

If you've never made anything bread-y before, now is the time. Whip up a pizza, or spend an afternoon checking in on your first dough baby. Bread making, with a bit of practice, is deeply enjoyable. Use active dry yeast in a 1-pound (450 g) bag and store it in the freezer.

Ice Cream

Always hidden at the back of my freezer, under a bag of bread butts for making bread crumbs, is a pint of ice cream. My grandmother used to say, "A wantless creature won't survive," and sometimes I want ice cream.

TOOLS AND EQUIPMENT

[C] When it comes to kitchen equipment, I am in the minimalist camp. A few well-cared-for, good-quality items are all you need to cook excellent food. If you don't have some of the items mentioned below, that's okay. You can always invest when you're ready and use what you currently have in the meantime. Another great option is to purchase gently used items, either online or from a thrift store.

Very Large Stockpot with Lid

This item is a must-have for soups, stews and braises, and it's also great for sterilizing bottles (and those soothers that constantly seem to be hitting the floor). When the girls were babies and I renovated my home and there was no hot water, I also used a stockpot to warm bathwater for all of us. You never know when a big pot will be very useful.

Large Cast Iron Pot or Enamel Dutch Oven

Our most used piece of kitchen equipment. It's stovetop ready, oven safe and can be used for storing and reheating later on. Great for braising meat and then finishing it in the oven, or if you're short on bowls, it can be used to store a rising bread dough in a pinch.

Medium Saucepan

An 8-inch (20 cm) saucepan with a fitted lid is just the thing to cook a pot of rice, warm a bottle of milk or heat up dinner for two. Look for a level bottom and be sure the lid fits tightly with no gaps.

Large, Deep Cast Iron Skillet

Use daily to reheat leftovers and sear veggies and meats before finishing them in the oven.

Small Ceramic Skillet

I shy away from Teflon, but ceramic has all the non-stick qualities without the polytetrafluoroethylene, which releases toxic chemicals at high temperatures. A small size—8 inches (20 cm)—is just right for one egg, a few pancakes or a delicate piece of fish.

Rimmed Baking Sheets

My house is old and everything is on an angle, including my oven. Rims keep roasting juices from dripping and spattering, cookies from sliding to a fiery death and granola from spilling everywhere when I try to toss it.

Loaf Pan

For loaf making.

Metal Bowls

One large bowl for baking; one medium bowl for mixing dressings or salads.

Microplane

An essential tool for getting every bit of zest off a lemon or finely grating cheese into pastas and soups.

Box Grater

A big, clunky grater is useful for shredding soft cheeses like mozzarella but also for grating zucchini for a Cool Hand Zucc (page 108) or even frozen butter for Flakey Biscuits (page 39).

Bench Knife

Cooking is so much better with a bench knife. Don't be deceived by the name—this is not actually a knife, but a dull metal blade with a handle on one side. Use it to scrape chopped veggies into a pot, wipe sticky herb bits off a knife, "cut" through cheeses or butter or scrape play dough off counters. It's a cheap tool but worth every penny. Look for one at any kitchen supply store—once you start using it, you'll never go back.

Metal, Wooden and Rubber Spatulas

The trifecta! Get a good, flexible perforated fish spatula at a kitchen supply store and use it for everything from frying eggs to lifting cookies to flipping pancakes. A wooden spatula is basically a wooden spoon with a flat bottom and is great for stirring onions, making a roux or mixing doughs. A rubber spatula is indispensable for getting every last bit of whatever you are making out of its cooking vessel and into its final destination.

Balloon Whisk

Emma was intrigued by the size of my whisk during our prepartum cook-off. "It's so big!" she declared. "Should I have a whisk that big, too?" The answer is yes. The bigger the whisk, the less work you have to do to make fluffy scrambled eggs or a well-combined dressing. I like one that is 3 inches (8 cm) in diameter. However big your whisk, just be sure you use a bowl commensurate with its size—large whisk, large bowl.

Blender and/or Food Processor

If you have the space and budget for a high-speed blender, it can be an extremely useful piece of equipment. If not, a sturdy Oster or Cuisinart model will still get the job done. A food processor can be useful, especially for making nut butters and dips, but is by no means essential.

Stand Mixer or Hand Mixer

I do not own a stand mixer, but this is another add-on you may want to buy if you really get the baking bug. I use a wooden spoon or spatula because I like the arm workout, but do whatever works for you.

CRAVINGS

The part when you're pregnant and revelling in highly specific food hankerings.

[E] This chapter is about eating during pregnancy. It's not about what you *should* eat, because you're likely fielding more than enough unsolicited opinions about that just now, but rather what you might like to eat. If we could open a restaurant for pregnant women and their people, this would be the menu: comfort food classics that satisfy some of the most common pregnancy cravings, but are equally craveable if you're not pregnant.

While the baby lives inside you, your food needs are aligned: if it asks for Cacio e Pepe (page 54), or French Onion Soup with Cheese Toast (page 37), or Chocolate Sheet Cake with Sour Cream Frosting (page 61), who are you to stand in its way? It becomes more complicated when the child's needs are (temporarily) expressed in shrill wails that don't result in you getting to eat cake, so seize this opportunity while it's there.

[C] Early in my pregnancy I was trying—hard—to get all of my essential vitamins and minerals and whatever else in the form of a giant pink (why always pink?) prenatal vitamin. I took one every morning with a meal, until one day my snooze button trumped my morning routine. Late for work, I threw on some clothes, dry-swallowed the horse pill of a vitamin and then, remembering that it's fat soluble, took two swigs of olive oil from the bottle and sprinted to the streetcar. In retrospect, it probably wasn't quite a sprint, but it was as fast as I could move, and my feeling of relief at making my ride was almost immediately overwhelmed by a wave of pure nausea.

With one hand clutched over my mouth and the other scrabbling at the doors, I yelled, "STOP!" and proceeded to stumble out onto the street at 9:15 AM and horrify innocent pedestrians.

"Don't worry!" I dry-heaved, waving an arm at no one in particular, "I'm pregnant!"

I've been incapable of taking another vitamin since. This caused me great worry until one day I Googled sources of folic acid, fearing that I might not be getting enough of this crucial-during-pregnancy B vitamin. The results: bread, pasta, beans, citrus, dark leafy greens. More or less an ingredients list of my diet over the previous weeks. From that day on I trusted what my body was hungry for and enjoyed cooking—selecting my ingredients with care and making exactly what I wanted—more than ever before in my life.

For me, these recipes are like a greatest hits album, not because they are technical or elaborate, but because they can be prepared without too much fuss and will taste very good when you're pregnant. But you can also return to them again and again, whenever you crave them.

REALLY CRUNCHY GRANOLA

Makes 4 cups (1 L)

[C] When I was pregnant, I wanted a lot of things—cold fruit, burgers, sheet cake—but most of all I wanted CRUNCH. I made this recipe frequently and ate large bowls of it with very cold Vanilla Almond Milk (page 20), on top of yogurt and berries—and also by the fistful to crunchify the pints of ice cream I was eating on a *very* regular basis.

¼ cup (60 mL) cashew butter

¼ cup (60 mL) honey

¼ cup (60 mL) coconut oil

½ teaspoon (2 mL) pure vanilla
extract

2 cups (500 mL) rolled oats

½ cup (125 mL) unsweetened
shredded coconut

¼ cup (60 mL) millet

¼ cup (60 mL) raw almonds,
chopped

¼ cup (60 mL) raw sunflower
seeds

½ teaspoon (2 mL) salt

Preheat the oven to 325°F (160°C).

In a small saucepan over medium-high heat, stir to combine the cashew butter, honey, coconut oil and vanilla.

In a large bowl, combine the rolled oats, coconut, millet, almonds, sunflower seeds, and salt. Add the cashew butter mixture to the bowl and stir until the oat mixture is evenly coated.

Spread the granola in an even layer on a baking sheet. Bake for 10 minutes. Remove the granola from the oven and stir. Bake for 8 minutes. Remove from the oven again and reduce the temperature to 300°F (150°C). Stir the granola and return it to the oven for an additional 5 minutes, or until the coconut turns golden brown.

To ensure that any leftover granola remains crunchy, let it cool to room temperature before transferring it to an airtight container. Store the granola at room temperature.

TIP: If you don't have millet, go ahead and sub in an equal amount of quinoa.

VANILLA ALMOND MILK

Makes about 2 cups (500 mL)

[E] This is our beverage company Greenhouse's old-school almond milk, which was basically an almond milkshake. To make this less like a milkshake and more like the kind of almond milk you'd use in a smoothie or another recipe, go dateless and omit the coconut oil.

1 cup (250 mL) raw almonds
4 Medjool dates, pitted and chopped
1 teaspoon (5 mL) pure vanilla extract
1 tablespoon (15 mL) coconut oil
Pinch of salt
3 cups (750 mL) filtered water, divided

In a medium bowl, soak the almonds in hot water for 10 to 20 minutes or in cold water overnight. Drain and rinse.

In a blender, combine the almonds, dates, vanilla, coconut oil, salt and 1 cup (250 mL) of the water. Blend on low until combined. Add the remaining 2 cups (500 mL) water to the blender and blend for 1 minute, or until smooth.

Place a large sieve lined with 2 layers of cheesecloth over a large bowl. Pour half of the mixture into the centre of the cloth, gather it into a pouch and squeeze the nut milk into the bowl. Repeat with the rest of the mixture.

Serve the milk very cold. Store in an airtight jar in the fridge for up to 3 days.

TIP: If you don't have cheesecloth, you can press the mixture through a fine mesh sieve into a large bowl with a spoon or spatula. Save the solids and add them to oatmeal or a smoothie.

COLD FRUITS SMOOTHIE BOWL

Makes 1 large bowl or 2 smaller ones

[E] Christine craved cold fruits while she was pregnant. I found fruits and vegetables repugnant for three months, which was awkward because I co-own a juice company. This is an adaptation of one of our smoothie bowls, the Blueberry Crumble Bowl, and it works for fruit-cravers, fruit-and-vegetable evaders and everyone in between. It's cold and sweet but also nutty and oaty, and you can stuff in a handful of spinach or kale without changing the taste (although the colour will be less attractive). Frozen raspberries add hits of tartness, and the more toppings, the better.

1 frozen banana, roughly chopped (see Tip)

½ cup (125 mL) frozen blueberries

¼ cup (60 mL) frozen raspberries (optional)

Handful of kale or spinach (optional)

1 tablespoon (15 mL) rolled oats

1 tablespoon (15 mL) almond butter or nut butter of choice

1 teaspoon (5 mL) pure vanilla extract

1 cup (250 mL) Vanilla Almond Milk (page 20) or nut or oat milk of choice, plus more if needed

TOPPINGS

Handful of Really Crunchy Granola (page 19), frozen berries, pumpkin seeds, hemp hearts and/or unsweetened shredded coconut

Drizzle of melted nut butter and/or Raspberry Chia Jam (page 257)

To make the smoothie bowl, place all ingredients (except the toppings) in a blender. Blend on low until loosely combined and then on high until smooth, about 30 to 45 seconds. If your ingredients aren't blending properly, turn off the blender, stir the mixture with a rubber spatula and add another ¼ cup (75 mL) almond milk or water. Blend again.

Transfer the smoothie to a wide bowl. Add desired toppings. Serve immediately.

TIP: If your cold fruit craving comes on at a moment when you don't have any bananas in the freezer, don't fret! Use a room-temperature banana instead and add ½ cup (125 mL) ice cubes to the blender along with the rest of the ingredients before you start blending. The texture won't be quite as creamy, but it will still be delicious.

CHOOSING MOTHERHOOD

[E] I found out on a Wednesday in June. On the following Sunday morning, I was staring at the bathroom mirror when I got Christine's text. She had spent her Wednesday in the hospital, having twins. Now they were all home. Everyone was fine. Tired but fine, and relatively unscathed, considering.

Unencumbered by any sense of what's right and proper in these situations, I invited myself over. I needed to see Christine, to hear what she had been through and to meet her daughters. I remember thinking it was strange to joke with her by text when she had just done this powerful, terrifying thing. But Christine could make you chuckle during an asteroid shower, so I believed her when she said, yes, sure, come by.

On my way over, I stopped at a nearby Polish restaurant and ordered a dozen cheddar and potato pierogies to go, with all the fixings. Then I went to the ice cream shop, waited in line with all the kids in the neighbourhood, and got myself a chocolate cone, which I ate standing in front of the shop, rushing to stay ahead of the melt.

Anthony and I were already, along with another partner, Hana, the over-extended parents of a three-and-a-half-year-old business. Thanks to a colossal loan, we were about to open a new beverage plant with enormous capacity and overhead costs to match. Anthony and I had discussed trying to start a family later, once we had brought the company to a place of greater safety and could come up for air.

When I arrived at Christine's place above the knitting shop, pierogies in hand, the dogs greeted me waggily. There she was, in the sunken living room looking exactly like herself, one baby sleeping in her arms, the other in a bassinet on the desk by the window.

"You're not supposed to put those things on tables," she told me. "But she's not going anywhere."

I took a baby in my arms. It was Matilda. She was light and warm and sweet-smelling. As I held her, and then continued to hold her well past the end of the acceptable new mother visitation window, the question I'd been torturing myself with for the past few days receded. My perspective, which for years had been narrowly trained on the insides of our small business, shifted. I could clearly see my friend Christine—a smart, hard-working, self-sufficient businessperson and chef—and the two tiny people she had made (plus dogs): her family.

I eventually shook myself out of my trance and gave Christine her daughter back. Walking home past the Ice Queen Restaurant and T Dot Jerk, toward the lake and up Queen Street, I realized what I had done. It wasn't the imposition on Christine, who had just given birth twice and didn't need me in her living room for two hours. That I didn't grasp for another eight months or so. What I suddenly understood was that I had made a decision hours earlier. By inviting myself over, by stepping into Christine's new world, I had chosen the path my body had started on—a few years early. I had chosen motherhood.

WEDGE SALAD WITH GREEN RANCH AND PICKLES

Serves 4

[C] What can I say about iceberg lettuce, except that it is highly, highly underrated? How did this happen? Why the lack of respect for this absolutely charming character in the produce aisle? It's such a useful lettuce and had so many of the qualities I was looking for in produce during my second and third trimesters—crunchy, refreshing, you can wrap stuff in it, and so on. Move over mesclun, because here is a salad that truly celebrates the very essence of iceberg; it's dead simple but highly craveable: the wedge!

PICKLED ONIONS

1 cup (250 mL) thinly sliced red onions

½ cup (125 mL) Pickling Liquid (page 253)

WEDGE SALAD

1 small head iceberg lettuce, cut into 4 wedges, core removed

1 cup (250 mL) loosely packed crumbled Stilton blue cheese

3 to 4 slices fresh thick-cut bacon, crisped and chopped (optional)

3 to 4 vine-ripened tomatoes, chopped

½ cup (125 mL) pickled onions

1 cup (250 mL) Green Ranch (page 265)

6 chives, finely chopped

To make the pickled onions, place the onions in a small heatproof container with a lid.

Pour the hot pickling liquid over the onions and cover. Let the onions cool to room temperature in the liquid. Once they have turned bright pink, they are ready to use.

To assemble the wedge salad, arrange each wedge of lettuce on a plate. Top each with an equal amount of cheese, bacon (if using), tomatoes and pickled onions. Drizzle ¼ cup (60 mL) Green Ranch over each wedge and sprinkle the chives on top.

TIP: You can plate this salad individually as pictured, but anytime I can platter, I usually do. It saves time on being too fussy, since plattered foods always look delicious and abundant, and people get to choose what they want and scoop up as many good bits as they can.

CAESAR SALAD WITH GARLICKY CROUTONS

Serves 4 to 5 as a side

[C] I know we've all convinced ourselves that a kale Caesar with coconut bacon is somehow a Caesar salad, but it is not. Real Caesar salad is funky, sharp, crisp and has no bacon (not even of the coconut variety). It's good enough to eat as a meal, but also plays well with roasted chicken or fish, a simple omelette or grilled vegetables.

¾ cup (175 mL) extra-virgin olive oil

2 cloves garlic, smashed

½ loaf stale white bread

Salt and coarsely cracked black pepper

1 tablespoon (15 mL) prepared mayonnaise

2 teaspoons (10 mL) Worcestershire sauce

3 good-quality anchovies, roughly chopped

1 to 2 tablespoons (15 to 30 mL) capers

1 tablespoon (15 mL) Dijon mustard

Juice of 1 lemon

Splash of caper juice (optional)

1 cup (250 mL) finely grated Pecorino Romano cheese, divided

1 head romaine lettuce, washed, dried and torn into bite-size pieces

TIP: The croutons will fry even better if you cut or tear the bread the night before and spread it out on a baking sheet to dry out even more.

Place the olive oil and garlic in a small saucepan over high heat. Bring to just under a boil and turn off the heat. Let the garlic steep in the oil while you cut or tear the bread into 1-inch (2.5 cm) chunks. You're more than welcome to trim the crusts off, but I like to keep things rustic—plus, I'm way too busy to care about things like that (see Tip).

Transfer 4 tablespoons (60 mL) of the oil to a large cast iron skillet over medium-high heat and cook until just shimmering. Reserve the remaining oil for the dressing. Add the bread chunks to the skillet and cook, stirring gently, until all sides of the bread pieces are golden brown. Season with salt, to taste. Set aside to cool. These are the croutons for the salad.

In a high-speed blender, combine the mayonnaise, Worcestershire sauce, anchovies, capers, mustard, lemon juice and caper juice, if using. Pulse to combine. Add about half of the Pecorino and pulse until combined. With the blender on low speed, drizzle in the remaining garlic oil and blend until fully incorporated. If the dressing is too thick, add 1 to 2 tablespoons (15 to 30 mL) of water to thin it out, if desired.

Get out your largest bowl. (You'll need lots of room for tossing!) Place the lettuce in the bowl. Drizzle in about half of the dressing, add half of the remaining Pecorino cheese and toss until the lettuce is evenly coated. Add the remaining dressing, half of the croutons and a few cracks of black pepper and toss again until evenly coated. Top with the remaining croutons, Pecorino and lots of black pepper. Serve immediately.

SUMMER VEGETABLE SUCCOTASH

Serves 2 as a meal, 4 to 6 as a side

[C] I craved a lot of vegetables when I was pregnant, and this recipe is a real catch-all. It's best made at the height of summer with fresh fava beans, corn and tomatoes. I generally serve this recipe as a side, but it can easily be enjoyed as a whole meal alongside a fried egg or a creamy lump of burrata.

2 tablespoons (30 mL) unsalted butter

3 slices fresh thick-cut bacon

1 medium white onion, thinly sliced

2 ears corn, kernels removed and cobs discarded

1 cup (250 mL) shelled favas (see Tip)

Splash of white wine (optional)

½ cup (125 mL) grape tomatoes, halved

2 handfuls of baby arugula

Handful of basil, finely sliced

1 tablespoon (15 mL) sherry vinegar

Salt and pepper

In a large cast iron skillet, melt the butter over medium heat. Add the bacon and cook gently for 7 to 10 minutes, until the bacon is cooked but not crisp. Remove the bacon from the pan and set aside. Do not discard the bacon fat.

In the same skillet over medium heat, cook the onion in the bacon fat until soft, 7 to 10 minutes. Add the corn, favas and white wine (if using) and cook for 2 to 3 minutes, stirring occasionally. Add the tomatoes and arugula. Roughly chop the bacon and add it to the skillet. Turn off the heat. Add the basil and sherry vinegar and stir to combine. Sprinkle with salt and pepper, to taste. Serve hot.

TIP: If you've never shelled favas before, it's a two-step process. They come in giant pods, sort of like a downy sleeping bag, and once you pluck the favas out of there, you need to dunk them in a giant saucepan of boiling salted water for 1 to 2 minutes, then plunge them into a bowl full of icy water before taking the skins off. This is a bit of a task, but if you don't have children yet, it's manageable. I actually find this "kitchen chore" deeply enjoyable in a meditative sort of way.

CONSIDER THE OYSTER:
ON EATING, REGRET AND HOPE

[C] The email I received from Denis was clear and to the point. Four days. France. A dozen or so people wanted to experience the best of regional wine and food, and Denis needed help producing the tour. My role was simply to experience it right along with them, provided I could get myself there and was willing to set up and break down the events and occasionally corral someone who found themselves at the bottom of a magnum of Chassagne-Montrachet.

When I was twenty-seven, I'd lived with Denis for a month in Burgundy while working at a Michelin-star restaurant. It was a crazy time, working from 9 AM to 1 AM five or six days a week (unpaid), with a three-hour break (during which I slept) in the middle of each workday. I'd spent most of my time on menial cooks' tasks, scrubbing floors and chopping apples in a perfect dice. I'd had a cook's-eye view of the area, but never that of a tourist. This recent invitation was an opportunity I could not pass up. It was the chance to really *enjoy* French cuisine, not just toil over it.

Denis was true to his word, and the trip was *magnifique*. We rode around in a hulking Mercedes bus, pulling up to ancient castles to eat puffy golden gougères, quivering shellfish swimming in cream, rosy pink squab doused in a sauce made from puréed liver and chocolate confections that were like tiny pieces of art. Soft cheese, for which I have a weakness, followed. Once they've been wheeled out on a massive cart, it is hard to choose just one cheese when you're in France for a good time, not a long time. Tongues wagging and eyes rolling in pleasure, everything was washed down with bottles of creamy white Burgundy, and just when we looked up at the clock and saw it was only 12:15 in the afternoon, the red wine came out. Later, we got back on the bus and went to dinner.

In a blur, it was over, and I lurched back into reality, which at the time felt kind of blah. The weight I'd put on in France showed no signs of leaving me, although to be fair, I'd been heavier than usual when I went.

At that time, I had no idea that I was pregnant, although you've probably already put it together—faster than I did. It would be another week or so before I did a mental count and realized that I was very, very late, and a few more days after that before I got up the nerve to take a pregnancy test (spoiler: it was positive) in the bathroom at work.

The anxiety of being unwed, not ready, kind of broke, and knowing I was going to become a parent was eclipsed by the more immediate and pressing worry that I had already damaged the fragile little fava bean-shaped person inside me. I booked the necessary appointments, and waddled my way around the city to have blood drawn and urine sampled. I cried and then laughed when the ultrasound tech flipped the monitor to show me not one but two black and white blobs. I could hear their heartbeats murmuring, but I could not tell if the carts of unpasteurized cheese had already wreaked havoc on their tiny world.

When I first met my OB-GYN, I was deeply uncomfortable. I was the only non-couple sitting in the waiting room, and the nurse was terse and to the point, qualities I wanted in the delivery room but not in a receptionist grilling me to see if I'd checked in correctly or brought the right paperwork (I had not). I was teary by the time Dr. B met me, overwhelmed not just by the nurse, but by everything, and wishing I'd brought someone along. Elderly and calm, he talked me through a lot of talk, and my blood pressure was high, but when he checked it again it had come down to *less* high. We warmed to one another, chatting about my work and our shared love of travel and food. He was planning a trip to Holland in the New Year, and the conversation turned to Gouda preferences (I love it when it's aged enough to get those crispy little crystals) and the merits of a good *bitterballen*.

At the end of it all, as he started shuffling out the door, I suddenly sat up and squeaked, "Dr. B?!" He turned, hand on the knob. "Is there anything I can't eat?" He removed his hand long enough to wave dismissively. "I've been doing this a long time. I don't really believe in all that. Eat what you want." So, there it was. I didn't ask for a second opinion.

In addition to putting up with the many tears I shed in his office, Dr. B gave me a gift that day. It wasn't the get-out-of-jail-free card for everything I'd put into my body in those early weeks, but the sense that everything would be *fine*. Not enough people tell you that when you're pregnant and yet it's the thing you need to hear the most. Dr. B taught me, gently but firmly, a lesson I have repeated to myself over and over again—that babies are resilient, and so am I.

FRENCH ONION SOUP WITH CHEESE TOAST

Serves 4 to 6

[C] When you're pregnant, it is absolutely the time to indulge in lengthy and somewhat involved cooking projects. You should spoil yourself, and you should eat what you want because that's likely going to change soon, and dramatically. This recipe takes a bit of prep and some cooking time, but I like to think of it as an investment, not just in a good soup, but in myself. Plus, there's cheese toast!

2 tablespoons (30 mL) unsalted butter

1 tablespoon (15 mL) olive oil

2½ pounds (1.125 kg) yellow onions, thinly sliced (about 6 medium onions)

Salt and pepper

1 cup (250 mL) dry red or white wine

4 cups (1 L) low- or no-sodium beef stock (see Tips)

Small handful of thyme

3 bay leaves

4 tablespoons (60 mL) cognac or Armagnac (optional)

4 to 6 slices stale, toasted baguette

4 to 6 slices Gruyère, Swiss or Emmental cheese

Trim a piece of parchment paper to fit in the bottom of a large Dutch oven and set the paper aside.

In the large Dutch oven, heat the butter and olive oil over medium heat, until the butter is melted. Add the onions and sprinkle with a pinch of salt. Place the parchment paper over the onions and press it down so that they really start to sweat and release their juices (see Tips). Reduce the heat to medium-low and cook for 40 minutes, or until the onions are very soft, lifting the parchment every 10 minutes or so to stir. Discard the parchment paper.

Crank the heat up to medium-high. Cook off all liquid in the Dutch oven and begin to brown the onions. Continue cooking for another 20 to 30 minutes, stirring just often enough so that the onions do not stick to the bottom, until they turn a deep golden colour. Once crusty bits start to develop on the bottom of the pot, add the wine and use a wooden spoon or spatula to scrape up all that good flavour. Continue cooking until the wine has reduced by half.

Add the stock to the onion mixture. Tie the thyme and bay leaves together with a piece of kitchen twine. Add the herb bundle to the stock. Bring to a boil and simmer, uncovered, for another 20 to 30 minutes.

Remove and discard the thyme and bay bundle. Add the cognac (if using) and season with salt and pepper, to taste.

continues

Preheat the broiler to high. Divide the hot soup among heatproof bowls. Place a slice of baguette and a slice of cheese on each. Place the bowls on a baking sheet and broil for 4 to 5 minutes, until the cheese is bubbling and brown.

TIPS: For a vegan version of this soup, you can make a deceptively delicious rutabaga stock that mimics the rich, deep flavour of a good beef stock. Simply make a standard batch of Vegetable Stock (page 254), substituting an additional 3 to 4 large rutabaga, cut into quarters, for the carrots.

If you don't want to bother covering the onions with parchment paper, it's not crucial; pop a lid on the Dutch oven instead so that the onions steam and sweat instead of simply roasting.

FLAKEY BISCUITS WITH SAUSAGE GRAVY

Serves 4

[C] This meal is stick-to-your-ribs carby, creamy and has just a whisper of Thanksgiving-y comfort to it. I keep it in my back pocket for rainy days or chilly evenings with people who, like me, are occasionally so moved by a meal that they quietly groan with pleasure while eating. Biscuits can seem intimidating, but my trick is to freeze the butter and grate it with a box grater to speed up the process and get an even distribution of butter.

BISCUITS

½ cup (125 mL) unsalted butter

2 cups (500 mL) + ¼ cup (60 mL)
   all-purpose flour, divided

1 tablespoon (15 mL) granulated
   sugar

1 teaspoon (5 mL) salt

4 teaspoons (20 mL) baking
   powder

1 teaspoon (5 mL) baking soda

½ cup (125 mL) whole milk

½ cup (125 mL) full-fat sour cream

SAUSAGE GRAVY

2 tablespoons (30 mL) unsalted
   butter

½ pound (225 g) breakfast
   sausage, casings removed

½ cup (125 mL) diced onion

1 teaspoon (5 mL) minced garlic

5 sage leaves, tied into a small
   bundle with kitchen twine

2 tablespoons (30 mL) all-purpose
   flour

2½ cups (625 mL) whole milk

1 tablespoon (15 mL) Dijon
   mustard

Salt and black pepper

Preheat the oven to 425°F (220°C). Place the butter and a box grater in the freezer.

To make the biscuits, in a large bowl, sift together 2 cups (500 mL) of the flour, sugar, salt, baking powder and baking soda. Once the butter is thoroughly chilled (about 15 minutes), place the grater in the bowl of dry ingredients and quickly grate in the butter. Stir until the butter is evenly dispersed in the flour mixture. Add the whole milk and sour cream and stir to combine. The dough will still be slightly sticky and shaggy, but it should form a large ball. Transfer the dough to a large clean surface, such as a cutting board or countertop, that has been liberally dusted with the remaining ¼ cup (60 mL) flour. Using floured hands, knead the dough until smooth.

Using your hands (not a rolling pin), flatten the dough into a large rectangle about 2 inches (5 cm) thick. Fold the dough in half. Repeat 4 or 5 times (this will give you a flakier biscuit). Finish by flattening the dough into a 2-inch (5 cm) thick rectangle. Transfer it to a large non-stick or parchment-lined baking sheet and chill in the freezer for 15 minutes.

Cut the dough into 4 equal squares. Return the dough to the baking sheet and bake for 18 to 20 minutes, or until the outside of the biscuits is golden brown.

continues

Meanwhile, make the sausage gravy. In a large, heavy-bottomed saucepan, melt the butter over medium-high heat. Add the sausage, using a wooden spoon to break up the lumps as it cooks. Add the onion and turn down the heat to medium-low, cooking until the onion is translucent. Add the garlic. Cook for an additional 1 to 2 minutes, stirring briskly. Add the sage. Sprinkle in the flour and increase the heat to medium. Cook for 1 to 2 minutes, stirring continuously so that nothing sticks to the bottom of the saucepan. Pour in the milk and cook for 10 to 15 minutes, until the gravy has reduced by a third and thickens. Stir in the mustard and turn off the heat. Season with salt and pepper, to taste.

Divide the biscuits among plates and top each with about ½ cup (125 mL) of gravy before serving.

TIP: Wrap the uncooked biscuit dough tightly in plastic wrap and freeze for up to 2 months. To bake from frozen, follow the recipe method, but add 3 to 5 minutes to the bake time.

A VERY GOOD HAMBURGER

Makes 4 hamburgers

[C] I don't eat much red meat, but something about having two humans using my body as a short-term rental unit turned me into a raging carnivore. I'd keep it light during the week with lots of greens, vegetables and sushi, but when Friday rolled around, I'd go all out. My friend Kris (now a new mother herself, but at the time just a truly loyal friend willing to hang out with a big, grumpy pregnant lady on a Friday night) would come over, and I'd slap together a token salad and then spend half an hour curating the perfect burger using the best ground beef I could afford. We'd find an '80s movie, open a bottle of Pinot noir, grab a roll of paper towels and hunker down for the evening. I didn't always love being pregnant, but I did love those evenings with Kris, and I still love a good burger.

1 pound (450 g) grass-fed,
   medium ground beef
Salt and pepper
2 tablespoons (30 mL) neutral oil,
   such as canola or grapeseed

FOR SERVING

4 slices American cheese
4 brioche buns or large toasted
   English muffins
4 tablespoons (60 mL) yellow
   mustard
4 slices beefsteak tomato,
   seasoned with a pinch of salt
4 tablespoons (60 mL) ketchup
4 to 8 slices dill pickle or sweet
   pickles
4 slices sweet onion, soaked in ice
   water for 5 minutes
4 medium butter lettuce leaves
2 tablespoons (30 mL) prepared
   mayonnaise or Aioli (optional,
   page 260)

Divide the beef evenly into 4 puck-shaped patties about 1 inch (2.5 cm) thick. Pat the meat dry with some paper towel and go ahead and whisper an affirmation to yourself that this is going to be the most incredible burger of your life. Season both sides of the patties liberally with about 1 teaspoon (5 mL) salt and a few grinds of pepper.

In a large cast iron skillet, heat the oil over high heat until just shimmering. Tip each burger into the oil away from you, so that the oil does not splash in your direction. Cook for about 2 to 4 minutes, until the burger starts to brown. Reduce the heat just slightly to keep the oil from smoking. Continue cooking for about 3 to 5 minutes and resist the temptation to peek or move the burger (yes, I understand the suspense, but trust me) so that an even crust forms. Flip the patties, being careful to flip them away from and not toward you. Increase the heat to high and repeat on the second side so that both sides are evenly seared. If you (like me) prefer your burger on the medium-rare side, pull it out of the skillet immediately and let it rest on a clean plate away from the heat. If you like it a little more done, let it rest in the skillet.

continues

Place a slice of cheese on each hamburger patty. Spread about 1 tablespoon (15 mL) mustard on the bottom of each bun and top with a slice of tomato (this is strategic, since if you put the tomato on top of the burger, everything ends up sliding everywhere and this is both inevitable and disappointing). Place one patty on top of each tomato slice and top with ketchup, pickles, onion and lettuce, if desired. Note that the order in which you add the toppings is, once again, important. It's like BEDMAS (remember that essential acronym from high school math class?): you don't have to understand it, but you do have to follow the order of operations to ensure success. Spread the top half of each bun with mayonnaise (if using) and place it on top of the burger. Serve immediately, with extra napkins.

WE NEED TO TALK ABOUT JUNO

[E] A baby is like a houseguest who decides to renovate. It's particularly hard early on, when the changes are structural and the news might not be out. The prospect of having a real houseguest during this time, a teenaged French boy called Paul-Emile, made me nervous.

Paul-Emile had just graduated from high school. He was coming to spend a few weeks in Toronto to learn about our beverage company before starting business school in the fall.

"I can't even keep house plants alive," I had told our friend Sam, Paul-Emile's dad, by phone when we'd first discussed the idea of his coming to stay, well before pregnancy was on my summer itinerary.

"He's seventeen. He can keep himself alive," Sam had assured me.

By Paul-Emile's arrival, I was fourteen weeks along, and pregnancy was not becoming on me. Heavy-limbed and syrupy with exhaustion, seasick from morning to night with a tinny taste in my mouth that nothing could rinse out, puffier around the middle but not "showing," I was peevish.

I was especially irritable at work, and no one yet knew why. I once stepped out of a meeting "to take care of something," by which I meant fall asleep in the passenger seat of our car in broad daylight. I moved my desk to the window to get away from the smell of my teammate's tea, only to be assaulted by bus exhaust and cigarette smoke wafting up from the street.

"Oh, thank God," one colleague said when I eventually told her I was pregnant. "We thought you hated us."

Worse than the physical symptoms were the mental lassitude and emotional chaos. My body, busy performing one of nature's miracles, wasn't leaving my mind much energy to think through how in the world I was going to become a mother. I felt lazy and incompetent, which only exacerbated my fears about what was to come.

On the appointed Saturday night in July, we didn't know who to look for at baggage claim. It had been a decade since we'd last seen Paul-Emile. I had been nineteen then, at the beginning of my adult life, and he a small child. I circled a blond teenager in a hip-length tank top, discreetly at first, and then brazenly because his face was buried in his phone. Before I had a chance to swoop in and scare the flip-flops off the wrong kid, Paul-Emile, who looked the same as he had at six only taller, waved me down.

That night around the kitchen table, Anthony and I told Paul-Emile our news. I braced for an awkward silence, but he cried out in genuine delight, excitement bubbling over in the form of questions. Were we having a girl or a boy, when was she due, how big was she now, how did I feel? She was the size of a lemon, the internet told us. He named her Limonata, and she became his invisible little sister.

"Limonata doesn't want you to carry that," he'd scold on our long walks for provisions, taking the grocery bags from my hands.

One of the reasons I was uneasy about having a houseguest that summer was that I had an addiction I didn't want anyone to know about. While Anthony worked day and night getting our new factory up and running, if I wasn't at the office, or eating noodles, or sinking into our mattress like a thick layer of glue, I was watching the movie *Juno*.

Living vicariously through a quippy teen who gets pregnant, becomes her high school's *cautionary whale*—and stays resolutely herself throughout the transformation—was calming. In some ways, being pregnant was adolescence revisited. Once again, my hormones were visible to all, making a spectacle of the most private changes. The horror of that was somewhat assuaged by watching a fictional character deal with both at the same time—and pull it off.

At first, I tried to hide this habit from our guest. When a young person arrives in an adult's home, I recognized, it is best not to show him that you're addicted to watching a movie about a pregnant teen, however original the screenplay. I tried my best to be nurturing, to put his needs first.

"Are you practising on me?" he once asked, after I tried to serve him thirds at breakfast. But I couldn't hide my condition for long.

"Have you seen the movie *Juno*?" I asked casually after an early dinner one night, while Anthony was still at the plant. He hadn't. I made gigantic bowls of popcorn as a bribe. He laughed politely, and I tried not to lip sync along with the dialogue.

The next evening, perhaps realizing what he was dealing with, Paul-Emile cooked for me. He made me the top dish in his young repertoire: chicken and zucchini over brown rice. He had shopped and everything.

Trying to re-establish my position as the adult, I peppered him with maternal questions about his friends, his studies, his plans for the future. After dinner, we made popcorn again, and I passed him the remote. "Your turn," I said with all the selflessness of a soon-to-be mother.

"But you want to watch *Juno* again," he told me.

And so, we did.

Pregnant Lady TV Guide

In case *Juno* isn't all you need, here's our list of things to watch while you're pregnant and/or nursing all day. Control the remote while you can.

[E] **Everything by Nora Ephron and Nancy Meyers**
Surely this is obvious and requires no explanation. *You've Got Mail*, *When Harry Met Sally*, *Sleepless in Seattle*, *The Holiday*, *It's Complicated*. All involve adults who are still growing up, which is comforting.

Workin' Moms
Created by and starring the younger sister of *Juno*'s director, Catherine Reitman (what a family), this show took me by surprise from the first episode. It goes there.

Gilmore Girls
Okay, okay, say what you want. Give a pregnant lady a few squares of dark chocolate, a litre of sparkling water and a show about a mom and daughter who are best friends, drink a lot of coffee and have long-simmering romances with handsome English teachers and Dean Moriarty types? I'm going to watch that.

[C] *Call the Midwife*
Not just a pregnant recommendation, but for those first few weeks of intense feedings when you are half-animal, half-human, you'll need something to watch. I spent hours propped up among couch cushions watching CTM, marvelling at the wonder of birth while sipping hot tea and the occasional gin and tonic, frequently moved to tears.

Top Chef
Reality cooking shows are my bread and butter. I have watched every season of *Top Chef* multiple times (I believe I'm what's referred to as a "superfan"), and I still learn new things and am endlessly entertained. The ingredients, the challenges, the competitors and the host, Padma Lakshmi, all combine to make this show not just watchable but craveable.

LOADED SHEET PAN NACHOS

Serves 1 (Just kidding. It should probably serve 4 to 6, but you do you.)

[C] We would be remiss in writing a pregnancy cravings chapter if we didn't include nachos. Crunchy, spicy, creamy, cheesy, pickle-y. What else could you possibly want? For the record, I'm not suggesting pickles because it's a stereotype that pregnant women crave them, I'm suggesting them because they are delicious. Put them anywhere there's hot sauce; they make everything better. And every human growing another human deserves to eat nachos, so don't skimp on the cheese.

4 to 5 cups (1 to 1.25 L) good-quality corn chips (see Tip)

1 bunch scallions, ends trimmed and thinly sliced

2 tomatoes, diced

1 jalapeño pepper, thinly sliced

7 ounces (200 g) shredded Monterey Jack or mozzarella cheese

½ cup (125 mL) full-fat sour cream

1 avocado, pitted, peeled and diced

1 cup (250 mL) shredded iceberg lettuce (or "shrettuce," as I like to call it)

½ cup (125 mL) diced dill pickle

1 ear corn, kernels removed and cobs discarded

½ cup (125 mL) chopped cilantro

2 limes, cut in half

FOR SERVING

Hot sauce

Good-quality salsa

Preheat the oven to 400°F (200°C).

Spread half of the corn chips in an even layer on a large baking sheet. In a small bowl, combine the scallions, tomatoes and jalapeño. Sprinkle half of the mixture evenly over the chips, followed by half of the cheese. Arrange the remaining corn chips in an even layer on top, and sprinkle with the remaining scallion mixture and cheese.

Bake for 8 to 10 minutes, until the cheese is completely melted. Remove from the oven. Dollop sour cream liberally over the nachos. Top evenly with the avocado, lettuce, pickle, corn and cilantro. Squeeze the limes over top. Serve immediately and eat with gusto.

TIP: Use a sturdy corn chip. I tried to make these with a thin chip once, but they shattered under the weight of all the magnificent toppings and left me frustrated and hungry.

EGGPLANT PARMESAN

Makes 1 (9- × 13-inch/3.5 L) casserole

[C] This recipe title is a bit of a misnomer, since I have it on good authority from my friend Dave, whose grandma was from Calabria, that the only real way to make this is to use Pecorino Romano cheese—Parmesan's sheepier, saltier cousin. He also expressly forbade me from including mozzarella in any form and, of course, I like to use two kinds.

4 medium eggplants

6 eggs

2 tablespoons (30 mL) salt, divided, more for seasoning

1 cup (250 mL) all-purpose flour

Olive oil, for frying

2 cups (500 mL) shredded Pecorino Romano or Parmesan cheese

1 cup (250 mL) shredded mozzarella

2½ to 3 cups (625 to 750 mL) good-quality marinara sauce, divided

1 ball buffalo mozzarella (approximately ½ cup/125 mL)

Small handful of fresh basil (approximately ½ cup/125 mL)

Preheat the oven to 375°F (190°C). Line a large baking sheet with a few layers of paper towel.

Cut 2 eggplants, lengthwise, into ½-inch (1 cm) slices. Cut 2 eggplants, crosswise, into ½-inch (1 cm) slices.

Crack the eggs into a medium bowl. Add 1 tablespoon (15 mL) of the salt and whisk to combine. Place the flour in a second medium bowl. Add the remaining 1 tablespoon (15 mL) salt and whisk to combine.

Set a large cast iron or stainless steel skillet over medium-high heat. Pour olive oil into the skillet to a depth of about ½ inch (1 cm). Once the oil begins to shimmer, begin frying the eggplant in batches: toss a few eggplant slices (or enough to fill the skillet) in the flour mixture. Shake off the excess before dipping each slice in the egg mixture. Fry until golden brown on each side, about 1 to 2 minutes per side. Place the cooked eggplant on the prepared baking sheet to drain. Repeat with the remaining eggplant. Once you've fried all of the eggplant slices, season with salt, to taste.

In a small bowl, combine the shredded Pecorino and shredded mozzarella cheese. Spread about ½ cup (125 mL) of the marinara sauce in the bottom of a 9- × 13-inch baking dish. Arrange eggplant rounds in a single layer in the bottom of the baking dish. Top with ½ cup (125 mL) of the marinara sauce and about 1 cup (250 mL) of the cheese mixture. For the next layer, use the long eggplant shapes (alternating between round and long slices will help with structural integrity!), then top with ½ cup (125 mL) of the marinara sauce and 1 cup (250 mL) of the cheese mixture.

Continue to layer the eggplant with the sauce and the cheese mixture (do not put any of the cheese mixture on top), adding 2 more layers and making sure to alternate between round and long slices. Bake for 45 minutes, until the casserole is bubbling and the eggplant is tender. Turn off the oven but keep it closed to hold the heat.

Slice the buffalo mozzarella into ½-inch (1 cm) slices and arrange them in a single layer on top of the casserole. Return the casserole to the hot oven for 5 minutes, or until the buffalo mozzarella is melted.

Tear the basil into pieces and sprinkle evenly on top. Let cool for 10 to 15 minutes before serving. Store leftovers, covered, in the fridge for up to 1 week.

TIP: Eggplant Parmesan is just as delicious (and arguably even better) served cold the next day.

SPICY NOODS

Serves 4 to 6

[C] I fell in love with Thai cuisine when I went backpacking in Thailand years ago. The food was so in balance—packed with cooling fresh herbs, bright lemongrass, fiery chilies and salty fish sauce. When I was pregnant, I often got cravings for spicy food, and for spicy noodles in particular. Loosely inspired by Pad Thai and my favourite Thai flavours, this recipe requires a bit of prep, but it's definitely worth it.

½ pound (225 g) rice stick or pad thai noodles

4 tablespoons (60 mL) grapeseed or canola oil, divided

3 eggs, beaten

2 cloves garlic, minced

1-inch (2.5 cm) piece fresh ginger, peeled and minced

2 stalks lemongrass, smashed and bottom 2 inches (5 cm) thinly sliced

1 pound (450 g) bean sprouts

½ cup (125 mL) sweet chili sauce

½ cup (125 mL) water

¼ cup (60 mL) fish sauce

2 tablespoons (30 mL) sesame oil

Zest and juice of 2 limes, more juice to finish (optional)

1 red bird's eye chili, thinly sliced

½ cup (125 mL) thinly sliced scallions

Large handful of fresh cilantro, chopped, more for garnish

Small handful of fresh basil, chopped

½ cup (125 mL) unsalted cashews, chopped

FOR SERVING

Hot sauce such as Sriracha or sambal oelek

Lime wedges

Bring a large pot of water to a boil. Cook the noodles according to package instructions, less 2 minutes, so they remain al dente. Drain and spread out the noodles on a large baking sheet to cool.

Place 2 tablespoons (30 mL) of the oil in a large wok or skillet and heat on medium-high heat until it shimmers. Add the eggs and cook for about 1 to 2 minutes, until just slightly underdone and not fully set. Transfer the eggs to a large plate.

Add the remaining 2 tablespoons (30 mL) of oil to the same wok or skillet and reduce the heat to low. Add the garlic, ginger and lemongrass, and cook until the flavours start to release, about 3 to 4 minutes. Increase the heat to medium-high and add the bean sprouts, cooking until soft, about 3 to 4 minutes. Transfer the bean sprouts to the large plate with the eggs.

In the same wok or skillet, add the sweet chili sauce, water, fish sauce, sesame oil, lime zest and juice, and bird's eye chili. Bring to a boil and cook for 2 minutes over high heat. Add the noodles and return the bean sprouts and eggs to the wok or skillet, stirring until everything is evenly coated. Continue cooking until the noodles remain saucy but are not wet. Remove from the heat. Add the scallions, cilantro, basil, more lime juice (if using) and cashews. Stir to combine. Divide the noodles among bowls. Garnish with more cilantro and serve immediately with hot sauce and fresh lime wedges.

CACIO E PEPE

Serves 3 to 4

[E] *Cacio* is cheese, *pepe* is pepper and this pasta is heaven. Nutty, salty Pecorino pairs with starchy pasta water to coat your noodles, and freshly ground pepper keeps every bite exciting. Anthony does not cook indoors often, but when he does, he makes this, and he makes it beautifully. Stove-shy partners everywhere, this one's for you.

Salt

1 pound (450 g) fresh bucatini or spaghetti (dried works too)

3 tablespoons (45 mL) unsalted butter, divided

2 teaspoons (10 mL) freshly cracked black pepper, more to finish

1½ cups (375 mL) finely grated Pecorino Romano cheese, more to serve

Fill a large pot with water. Bring the water to a boil and salt it until it tastes like the sea. Cook the pasta according to package instructions, less 2 minutes; you will finish cooking it in the butter, cheese and pasta water and serve it al dente. Reserve 1½ cups (375 mL) of pasta water. Drain the pasta.

In a medium cast iron skillet, melt 2 tablespoons (30 mL) of the butter over medium-high heat. Add the pepper and cook for 1 minute.

Add the pasta and ½ cup (125 mL) of the reserved pasta water. Stirring, let the water simmer and reduce until it just coats the pasta, about 1 minute. Reduce the heat to medium-low and sprinkle on ½ cup (125 mL) of cheese, tossing constantly with tongs to coat the pasta evenly and melt the cheese. Once the cheese has melted, repeat with another ½ cup (125 mL) of pasta water and another ½ cup (125 mL) of cheese and continue tossing until the water has reduced and the cheese has melted. Add the remaining 1 tablespoon (15 mL) butter and toss with the remaining ½ cup (125 mL) cheese and another splash of pasta water, if needed, until the butter and cheese have melted and you have perfectly al dente noodles coated with a glossy layer of buttery, cheesy, peppery sauce. Add more pepper, to taste.

Divide the pasta among warm bowls and serve immediately with an extra dusting of cheese for good measure.

TOKYO TO THE MOON

[E] The second bowl of ramen was my favourite. In an unmarked basement in Kyoto, while young men in toques blowtorched leeks and slabs of pork belly behind the concrete bar, Anthony and I sat at the counter and slurped. A tangle of noodles with just the right bite, the spilling yolk of an *Ajitama* egg marinated in soy and mirin, a slowly simmered chicken broth that did not overpower its inhabitants and, for when the palate craved a change of scene, the sweet, smoky explosion of a cherry tomato.

I refilled my metal cup, cooling my throat. We bowed to the chefs, cut a path through the line for the vending machine where bowls are pre-ordered, and ceded our spots. No Name Ramen, the place was called. Clearly, it didn't need one.

Early in my first trimester, when every day felt like a bumpy bus ride, I learned a new word. Maybe you've heard it: *babymoon*. Although I could see the appeal of travelling with only hand luggage possibly for the last time ever, the idea of wilful displacement struck me as absurd. "We're not moon people," I told myself, swiping to the next listicle on my phone.

In the second trimester, though, once the nausea had faded and the news was out, new parents started pulling us aside and telling us things urgently. "Travel. NOW," many of them hissed. We hadn't taken more than a few consecutive days off since the launch of our business three and a half years prior. Our plan had once been to elope as soon as things calmed down, mainly as an excuse to visit Japan. I'd been dreaming of Japan for as long as I could remember, but it was far. Too far to go for a long weekend. Too far to go with a screaming baby, or a bigger child who costs a seat.

And then, when I was four months pregnant, Anthony was the one who pulled me aside. "I wanted to wait, but my sisters think you'd rather get these now," he said, handing me a stack of books: *Lonely Planet Kyoto*, *The Monocle Travel Guide to Tokyo*. "Thank you! I love Japan," I said, kissing him. He smiled, waiting. "HOLD ON—" I said. "DOES THIS MEAN—?" We left on my birthday.

"What about sushi?" a few hushed voices asked before our departure. Meaning, could I realistically abstain from raw fish, a Pregnancy Verboten List top-five item, in *Japan*? Walking the tightrope between the "how dare you risk the welfare of your unborn child" camp and the "relax and have a whisky" contingent, I answered in the same way I did the epidural question: "I'll play it by ear."

A different nervous bell went off in my head on the eve of our trip. I was now five months pregnant and needed to pee every eight minutes. That can really put a damper on a shrine visit. Anthony, who had been to Japan before, told me not to worry. Puzzlingly, he added, "You'll love the toilets."

Within hours of landing in Tokyo, I saw what he meant. We were in line for our first bowl of ramen (thick-cut "dipping" noodles) in an underground mall beneath Tokyo Station. I went off in search of a stick lady wearing a triangle dress. The toilets I found were equipped with buttons prompting music, flushing sounds (not to be confused with actual flushing) and many other functions I could not decipher. They were the hygiene equivalent of the computer operating system played by Scarlett Johansson's sexy voice in the movie *Her*. More importantly, they were everywhere.

We woke up at 4 AM and walked for thirty kilometres a day, in awe. It was over 30 degrees Celsius and I marched around in a T-shirt dress, socks and slip-on shoes and developed a close relationship with a soft drink called Pocari Sweat. I looked like I had escaped from a strange kind of spa, but I was having the time of my life.

The raw fish question turned out to be a red herring. Japan's culinary range is so vast that treating sushi FOMO as a real concern would be like wondering whether it would be worth the trip to Canada if one were allergic to maple syrup. There were cloud-like bites of lotus root at a tempura shop in Ginza. There was crispy, farm-to-table *tonkatsu* with shredded cabbage in the winding streets of Aoyama. There was teppanyaki with freshly grated wasabi in the food court of one of Marunouchi's gleaming office towers and an earthen pot of *yudofu*, a monk's meal of silken tofu cooked in broth, in the garden of a Zen shrine. And yes, there was some sashimi, lightly seared by a thoughtful chef named Shima. I only wished I were eating for more than two.

Toward the end of our trip we took a sightseeing boat ride down the Hozugawa River. "Your wife, is she pregnant?" the captain discreetly asked Anthony as he helped us into the rowboat. I was not his wife, but we grinned and nodded. We had gotten engaged just an hour before, and our giddiness must have been written all over us. A few times during the tour, which was conducted entirely in Japanese, the captain said something that made our fellow passengers look at us and erupt in laughter. We laughed with them. It was clear in any language: we were moon people now, and we loved it.

TOKYO

A very brief introduction

CHOCOLATE SHEET CAKE WITH SOUR CREAM FROSTING

Makes 1 (9-inch/2.5 L) square cake

[C] I baked a lot during my pregnancy. At a time when your body is huge and uncomfortable and you have little sense of control in your life, there's something reassuring about knowing that if you have butter, sugar, eggs and flour, you can whip up something that borders on extravagant "just because." There's also something extra comforting about chocolate cake (Nostalgia? Magnesium? Frosting?), so I suggest taking the time to indulge in a bit of self-care baking followed immediately by a bit of self-care eating.

CHOCOLATE CAKE

1½ cups (375 mL) all-purpose flour
1½ cups (375 mL) granulated
  sugar
½ cup (125 mL) cocoa powder
1½ teaspoons (7 mL) baking
  powder
1 teaspoon (5 mL) baking soda
Pinch of salt
¾ cup (175 mL) hot coffee
¾ cup (175 mL) full-fat sour cream
¼ cup (60 mL) virgin coconut oil,
  melted
1 teaspoon (5 mL) pure vanilla
  extract
2 eggs, beaten

SIMPLE SYRUP

½ cup (125 mL) granulated sugar
½ cup (125 mL) water
1 tablespoon (15 mL) Kahlua or
  other coffee-flavoured liqueur
  (optional)

Preheat the oven to 350°F (180°C). Grease a 9-inch (2.5 L) square cake pan.

To make the chocolate cake, in a large bowl, sift together the flour, sugar, cocoa, baking powder, baking soda and salt. In a medium bowl, combine the hot coffee, sour cream, coconut oil and vanilla. Quickly pour the hot liquid into the dry ingredients and whisk briskly for about 1 minute, until fully combined. Add the eggs and whisk again for an additional minute, until combined.

Using a rubber spatula, transfer the batter to the prepared cake pan and spread it in an even layer. Bake for 45 to 50 minutes, or until a toothpick inserted in the centre of the cake comes out clean.

While the cake is baking, prepare the simple syrup. Place the sugar and water in a small saucepan and bring to a boil over medium-high heat. Let boil for about 3 to 4 minutes, or until the syrup reduces by half. Remove the saucepan from the heat and let cool for 2 minutes. Add the Kahlua (if using) and whisk to combine. Set aside.

continues

SOUR CREAM FROSTING

¼ cup (60 mL) unsalted butter,
   softened
¼ cup (60 mL) full-fat sour cream
2 cups (500 mL) icing sugar
1 cup (250 mL) cocoa powder
Pinch of salt
2 tablespoons (30 mL) heavy
   cream
1 tablespoon (15 mL) rainbow
   sprinkles, for garnish (optional)

To make the sour cream frosting, in a large bowl and using a spatula, mix together the butter and sour cream. In a medium bowl, sift together the icing sugar, cocoa and salt. Using the spatula, slowly beat the dry ingredients into the butter and sour cream mixture until fully incorporated. Add the heavy cream 1 tablespoon (15 mL) at a time and continue beating until the frosting is smooth and spreadable.

When the cake is done, remove the pan from the oven and let cool for 5 to 10 minutes. Using a toothpick or skewer, poke a dozen holes in the top of the cake. Pour the warm simple syrup evenly over the top of the cake and allow it to soak in as it continues to cool. Let cool to room temperature.

Using a rubber spatula, scrape all of the frosting onto the middle of the cake. Run a large metal spoon under hot tap water for 1 minute. Dry the spoon and, while it is still warm, use it to swoosh the icing all over the top of the cake in an even layer. Garnish with the sprinkles, if using. Store the cake in an airtight container in the fridge for up to 5 days.

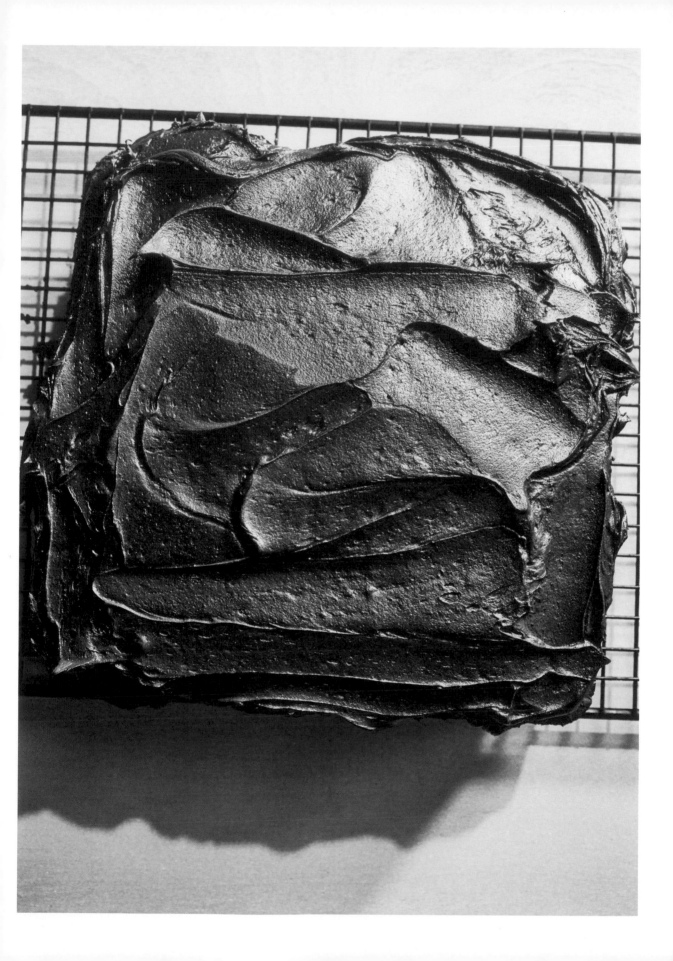

THE BIG CHILL

The part when birth is imminent and you're preparing yourself, mind, body, and freezer.

[C] I felt like a duck when I was pregnant. Not just because of my waddle, but because on the surface I was very calm (maybe too calm), while below the surface everything was churning and I was totally freaking out. My body was exploding, I was living in an apartment I knew I couldn't afford long term, I was working full time, and I was growing two humans. There were what felt like a million ways in which I couldn't control my situation; I was isolated, and I was scared. Cooking helped me feel better. A lot better.

So, at six months pregnant, I made my brother drive me to Costco, and I loaded up the cart with cans and cartons and chickens. I returned home, lugging groceries up my steep staircase, and spent two days listening to classic rock, rolling Polish Meatballs with Lemon and Caraway (page 93), braising Mexican Adobo with Pork and Chilies (page 81) and baking Chocolate Chip Banana Cake (page 98). I had a very small apartment freezer, but the meal prep was worth sacrificing a pint or two of Häagen-Dazs. As stressful as the first few weeks of being a mom were, I never had to worry about where my next meal was coming from.

When Emma told me she was pregnant, I was breastfeeding—in general and, likely, specifically at that time. As we texted back and forth, I felt a sense of sisterhood and an *obligation* to be genuinely helpful to someone who was going through what I had just been through. So, I offered to do the most useful thing I could think of.

[E] When I was eight months pregnant, Christine gave me a great present. She invited me to her house on a Sunday afternoon to show me how to give a baby a bath, and how to fill my freezer for the onslaught to come. Once Matilda was clean (Christine: "Piper doesn't love the bath—I don't want to scare you.") and the girls were comfy in their bouncy chairs, we made big batches of Golden Squash Soup (page 72), Chicken Noodle Soup, Sort Of (page 76) and Freezer Hummus (page 68) in the time it usually takes me to make dinner for two. I had never heard the term "flat-packing" before: we put everything in zip-top bags, pressed the air out and lay them flat, so that the contents would freeze in a thin layer for quick thawing. Squash soup from the top of my freezer stack was the first thing I ate as a mother.

HOW TO FREEZE AND THAW

[C] Freezing food properly makes a big difference. If you pack it flat in stacked, pre-labelled zip-top bags, your freezer will look neater, the food you want will be easier to find and it will thaw more quickly so there's less wait time between "hanger" and happy eating.

Freezer Meal Tips

For smoothie ingredients:
- Arrange fruits and vegetables in a single layer on a parchment-lined baking sheet and freeze, uncovered, for 15 minutes or so before transferring to zip-top freezer bags. This will help to keep ingredients from clumping together, which your blender will appreciate.

For braises, soups and stews:
- Chill in the fridge first, then portion into pre-labelled 1-gallon (4 L) zip-top bags and freeze for up to three months.
- To thaw, remove a zip-top bag from the freezer and place it in a large bowl in the sink. Run the bag under room-temperature water until you can easily remove the contents from the bag. (We wash and reuse our bags whenever possible, but it's a personal choice.)
- Transfer the contents of the bag to a saucepan and cook over medium heat, until the desired temperature is reached. Regardless of how "hangry" you are, do not heat your meal over high heat; the bottom will burn before the top gets a chance to warm through.

For individual items such as burger patties, chicken breasts and so on:
- Arrange items in a single layer on a parchment-lined baking sheet and freeze, uncovered, until just frozen.
- Pack into pre-labelled zip-top bags and return to the freezer for up to three months.
- To thaw, remove a bag from the freezer and place it in a medium bowl in the fridge.

For baked goods:
- You can freeze cookie dough (like the dough for 2 AM Cookies, page 158) flat in a zip-top bag, then roll it into balls from frozen (your hands will warm it up enough to roll) and bake it according to the recipe method.
- Portion out and freeze yeasted doughs, such as Pizza Dough (page 252) or bread dough (such as for Molasses Brown Bread, page 177), after the final rise. Thaw in the fridge overnight and let sit at room temperature for about 20 minutes before you bake according to the recipe method.
- Recipes like Flakey Biscuits (page 39) and Sour Cream Scones (page 97) can be shaped, frozen individually and packed in a zip-top bag. When it comes time to bake them, just follow the recipe method but add about 3 to 5 minutes to the bake time.

FREEZER HUMMUS

Makes 4 cups (1 L), or about 8 to 10 hearty portions

[C] It might seem strange, but hummus is a great food to pack your freezer with. If you pack it flat in a sturdy zip-top bag, it freezes (and thaws) quickly and takes up very little space. In this recipe, I add the chickpea liquid, known also as "aquafaba," to the hummus. It contains starch and helps make the hummus creamy and smooth. Dip your veggies in this hummus, spread it generously on some kind of delicious carb or dollop some on a quick fried egg. This recipe produces a very reasonable amount of creamy delicious hummus, but if you are really batch cooking, go ahead and double or triple it, as hummus is truly the queen of protein-packed, nourishing foods you can eat with one hand.

1 cup (250 mL) good-quality tahini

1 clove garlic

Zest and juice of 1 lemon

1 tablespoon (15 mL) kosher salt

½ cup (125 mL) ice water

½ cup (125 mL) extra-virgin olive oil, more for serving

2 cans (14 ounces/400 mL each) chickpeas, liquid reserved

Black and white sesame seeds, for serving (optional)

Place the tahini, garlic, lemon zest and juice and salt in a high-speed blender and pulse to combine. With the blender on low speed, slowly stream in the ice water to create a smooth paste. Increase the blender speed to medium. Stream in the olive oil and blend until fully combined. Add the chickpeas and blend until smooth and fluffy. Add the reserved chickpea liquid a splash at a time, continuing to blend on medium speed until all of the liquid has been fully incorporated and the hummus is smooth.

Drizzle with olive oil and sprinkle with sesame seeds, if desired. Serve with roasted veggies or slathered on a pita. Store leftovers in an airtight container in the fridge for up to 1 week or freeze in zip-top bags for up to 3 months.

PEACH GAZPACHO

Serves 4 to 6

[C] I love an ice-cold bowl of gazpacho, especially with a drizzle of olive oil and some crunchy croutons on top. Fresh peaches bring a touch of sweetness to this version and round out the acid from the tomatoes and vinegar, while helping to create a beautifully smooth texture. This soup is nutritionally dense and also has a good amount of healthy fats. For a heartier meal, it pairs well with charred bread and some white anchovies.

1 small clove garlic

1 small shallot

1 medium cucumber, ends trimmed and roughly chopped

2 red bell peppers, cored, seeded and roughly chopped

4 very ripe peaches, roughly chopped

5 vine or hothouse tomatoes, diced

¼ cup (60 mL) extra-virgin olive oil

1 tablespoon (15 mL) good-quality sherry vinegar

1 tablespoon (15 mL) granulated sugar or sweetener of choice (optional)

Salt and pepper

FOR SERVING

Extra-virgin olive oil

Garlicky Croutons (page 29)

Diced vegetables such as tomatoes, cucumbers and peppers

Diced avocado

Place the garlic, shallot, cucumber and peppers in a high-speed blender and pulse for about 1 minute. Take the lid off the blender and press everything down toward the blade with a wooden spoon. Add the peaches and tomatoes and purée on high speed until smooth. With the blender still running, drizzle in the olive oil and continue to purée on high until fully combined. Add the vinegar, sugar (if using) and salt and pepper, to taste. Pulse again for 30 seconds to combine.

For best flavour, refrigerate the gazpacho in an airtight container overnight and serve in chilled bowls with a drizzle of olive oil, a small handful of croutons and a few spoonfuls of diced vegetables and avocado.

Store the gazpacho (ungarnished) in an airtight container in the fridge for up to 5 days or freeze in zip-top bags for up to 3 months.

TIP: This is a wonderful meal to pull out of your freezer in the first few weeks of motherhood. Just thaw it, toss it back in the blender to re-blend, dump it in a glass and drink it like a savoury smoothie.

GOLDEN SQUASH SOUP

Serves 4 to 6

[C] Root vegetables, by their very nature, are grounding and extremely nourishing. This was one of the handful of recipes Emma and I cooked together during our prepartum prep, but I had no idea it would be the first thing she ate after giving birth. The soup heats up quickly from frozen and just needs a squeeze of lime and a splash of coconut milk to finish it off.

4 tablespoons (60 mL) virgin coconut oil

1 large onion, ends trimmed and quartered

1 small kabocha, acorn or butternut squash, peeled and cut into 1½-inch (3.5 cm) cubes (about 5 cups/1.25 L)

2 cloves garlic, smashed

1-inch (2.5 cm) piece fresh ginger, peeled and roughly chopped

2 stalks lemongrass, smashed and bottom 2 inches (5 cm) roughly chopped

1 teaspoon (5 mL) turmeric

4 cups (1 L) vegetable stock or water

5 dried kaffir lime leaves (see Tip)

2 tablespoons (30 mL) red curry paste

1 tablespoon (15 mL) granulated sugar

1 can (14 ounces/400 mL) full-fat coconut milk, more for garnish

3 tablespoons (45 mL) fish sauce

FOR SERVING
Freshly cracked black pepper
Lime juice

In a large stockpot, melt the coconut oil over medium-high heat. Add the onion and squash and cook, stirring frequently, for about 5 minutes so that they begin to soften. Add the garlic, ginger, lemongrass and turmeric and continue cooking for 2 minutes. Add the stock, lime leaves, curry paste and sugar. Cover, then reduce the heat to medium-low. Let simmer for 20 to 25 minutes, or until the squash is pierced easily with a paring knife. Pick out the lime leaves and discard. Let cool for 10 to 15 minutes.

Purée the soup in batches in a high-speed blender and return it to the pot. Stir in the coconut milk and fish sauce. Serve hot with a drizzle of coconut milk, cracked black pepper and a squeeze of lime juice.

Store the soup in an airtight container in the fridge for up to 1 week or freeze in zip-top bags for up to 3 months.

TIP: Kaffir lime leaves are one of my absolute favourite seasonings. If you can get them fresh, you're lucky, but you can find them dried in most Asian grocery stores or online.

YOU DON'T NEED EVERYTHING, BUT THESE THINGS ARE IMPORTANT

[E] As my due date neared, the idea of shopping for baby things inspired a feeling of cold panic. The internet told me I should be "nesting." I wasn't nesting at all. I was terrified of this becoming real, afraid I was running out of time to be me, the person I was used to being. I bristled at the mention of baby paraphernalia like the Grinch contemplating Christmas, until a snowy evening in mid-December when, at eight months pregnant, something in me shifted. I was suddenly compelled to march from work through the snow after dark to a toy store to fetch a regal, five-foot-tall stuffed giraffe I'd seen in the window. Gerald, I named him.

"Do you have a car?" the store owner asked as I dragged my final-sale cargo out the door. I brought Gerald on the bus at rush hour, his front legs straddling my enormous belly, his chin hanging over the hand rail. He made our fellow passengers smile, even as he stole precious inches of their personal space.

He lightened the mood for me, too. I realized that I wasn't going to have to build a new personality before giving birth; I could come as I was and figure it out as I went, carting my unwieldy baggage with me.

Two years later I climbed into Ezzie's crib in a desperate, method-parenting attempt to understand why she was so determined not to get into bed, and was surprised by how comforting it was to look up into Gerald's long-lashed gaze. "Ezzie, is it nice having Gerald watch over you while you sleep?" I asked, curling up in her fuzzy blanket shaped like a dog. "Yes," she said, looking at me curiously from the other side of the bars.

Gerald aside, here are some truly useful items for the baby phase:

- Doughnut-like pillow or clean dog bed for infant docking
- Bouncy chair (if you station it near where you're working, you can use one foot to bounce your baby into a dream state; we called this the "gas pedal" method)
- Baby carrier for walks and chores and general closeness and hands-freedom
- Cotton swaddles or burp cloths for days, because laundry for days
- Bra with holes where the nipples should be if you decide to pump (so you can read)
- Chair that rocks (literally and figuratively—for feeding, burping, passing out)
- Onesies with feet (if winter) that zip or tie kimono-style (snaps can be challenging in the dark)
- A mobile (not your phone, though they'll want that, too), because dangly things = hours of fun
- More food and water than you think is reasonable (for you)

CHICKEN NOODLE SOUP, SORT OF

Serves 8 to 10

[C] You *can* drop some egg noodles or broken spaghetti into your chicken noodle soup, or you can blow everyone's mind—including your own—and throw in some cheese tortellini at the end. Trust me, you will not regret this decision.

2 tablespoons (30 mL) olive oil

1 large onion, diced

4 carrots, diced

4 stalks celery, diced

10 cups (2.5 L) chicken stock

Small handful of fresh thyme, tied
    together with kitchen twine

Salt and pepper

4 cups (1 L) cooked chicken,
    chopped

FOR SERVING

2 pounds (900 g) cheese tortellini

Place the olive oil in a large stockpot over medium heat. Add the onion, carrots and celery and cook for 5 to 7 minutes, until the onions are translucent and the vegetables start to soften. Add the stock and thyme and increase the heat to high. Bring the soup to a boil. Reduce the heat to medium-low and let simmer, uncovered, for 15 to 20 minutes, or until the carrots are al dente. Remove the thyme bundle from the pot and discard. Season with salt and pepper, to taste. Add the chicken.

If you plan to serve the soup immediately, add the tortellini and cook for an additional 2 to 3 minutes. Store the soup in an airtight container in the fridge for up to 5 days.

If you want to save the soup for later, remove it from the stove, let cool to room temperature and freeze in zip-top bags for up to 3 months. Before serving, bring the thawed soup to a boil, add the tortellini and cook for 2 to 3 minutes.

TIP: For a greens boost, throw in 2 cups (500 mL) (or more!) of chopped hearty greens like chard, kale or collards when you add the tortellini.

RED BEET BORSCHT WITH CRÈME FRAÎCHE AND DILL

Serves 8 to 10

[C] If you have an oma, a bubbi, a babcia or a бабушка, chances are you've had a version of this soup. It's hearty, full of slow-braised meat and laced with chunks of root vegetables. Each bowlful is a treasure box of flavours and textures, with dark ruby coloured beets making it both luxurious and homey. In lieu of pork ribs, you can use beef ribs or other cheap braising cuts of beef and/or pork for this recipe.

BROTH

3 tablespoons (45 mL) neutral oil, such as canola or grapeseed
5 pounds (2.25 kg) pork ribs
Salt and pepper
2 medium onions, quartered
2 carrots, cut into 2-inch (5 cm) chunks
3 stalks celery, cut into 2-inch (5 cm) chunks
3 bay leaves
1 tablespoon (15 mL) whole black peppercorns
Fresh herb stems, such as flat-leaf parsley, dill and/or thyme (optional)
12 cups (3 L) chicken, beef or vegetable stock (homemade or low sodium)
2 cups (500 mL) water

BORSCHT

3 tablespoons (45 mL) neutral oil, such as canola or grapeseed
2 Spanish onions, diced
4 to 6 medium red beets, diced
4 large carrots, diced
½ small head Savoy cabbage, thinly sliced
2 to 4 cups (500 mL to 1 L) water
1 cup (250 mL) sauerkraut
Salt and pepper

Place a wire rack on top of a large baking sheet and set aside.

To make the broth, in a large Dutch oven, heat the oil over medium-high heat. Pat the pork ribs dry with paper towel and season generously with salt and pepper. Sear the ribs in batches and place them on the wire rack to drain (see Tip).

In the same Dutch oven, cook the onions, carrots and celery over medium heat for about 10 minutes, or until the onions soften, stirring often so that they do not brown. Drop in the bay leaves, peppercorns and herb stems, if using. Return the pork ribs to the pot. Add the stock and water and increase the heat to high. Bring the soup to a boil. Reduce the heat to medium-low and simmer for about 1½ to 2 hours, until the pork is falling off the bone.

Remove the soup from the heat and let cool for about 10 minutes. Gently pull out the bones and the meat and set aside to cool further. Using a fine-mesh sieve, strain the soup into a large container. Discard the solids. Once the pork is cool enough to handle, pick all of the meat from the bones and set aside. Discard the bones.

continues

FOR SERVING

Crème fraîche

Chopped fresh dill

Caraway seeds

To make the borscht, give the Dutch oven you used to make the broth a quick rinse. Add the oil to the Dutch oven and place it over medium-high heat. Once the oil starts to shimmer, add the onions and beets. Reduce the heat to medium and cook for about 5 minutes, or until the onions soften, stirring often so that they do not brown. Add the carrots and continue to cook, stirring often, for another 10 minutes. Add the cabbage and stir until it wilts, about 2 to 3 minutes.

Pour the water and broth into the Dutch oven with the vegetables. Increase the heat to high and bring to a boil. Reduce the heat to medium and simmer for 10 to 15 minutes, or until the beets are cooked through and can be pierced easily with a fork. Add the sauerkraut and braised pork. Continue cooking until the meat is heated through. Season with salt and pepper, to taste.

Serve the borscht hot with a dollop of crème fraîche, fresh dill and a sprinkle of caraway seeds. Store leftovers in an airtight container in the fridge for up to 5 days or freeze in zip-top bags for up to 3 months.

TIP: Anytime you plan to sear or caramelize meat, pull it out of the fridge an hour or two before, so it comes up to room temperature. Pat it dry to remove any moisture and ensure that your oil is shimmering before you lay the meat gently in the pan away from you—to make sure that any oil that splashes moves away from you, too. Finally, do not crowd the pan by adding too much meat at once, or the meat will steam instead of searing. Once you get that initial layer of sear after the first minute or so, reduce the heat to medium to build a deeper, darker crust.

MEXICAN ADOBO WITH PORK AND CHILIES

Serves 8 to 10

[C] I'm a Canadian who learned how to make this dish from my Chinese ex-boyfriend when I was in culinary school in New York. I absolutely cannot speak to the authenticity of the flavour profile, but I can tell you that it's delicious, it freezes well and it's one of my go-to dishes for feeding a large group when I'm on a budget (which is always). You want a well-marbled piece of meat for this recipe, since it is being braised. Look for a cut with an even distribution of white fat. The fat is full of vitamin D and will keep the meat moist as it cooks.

4 pounds (1.8 kg) bone-in pork shoulder or butt

1 tablespoon (15 mL) all-purpose flour

1 tablespoon (15 mL) kosher salt

1 tablespoon (15 mL) ground cumin

6 tablespoons (90 mL) neutral oil, such as grapeseed or canola, divided

1 medium yellow onion, thinly sliced

1 bunch fresh cilantro

4 cloves garlic, smashed

3 tablespoons (45 mL) tomato paste

1 can (28 ounces/800 g) whole peeled tomatoes

4 cups (1 L) chicken stock

1 or 2 chipotle peppers in adobo sauce (from 7-ounce/200 mL can), plus sauce

FOR SERVING

Cooked long grain rice

Lime wedges

Place a wire rack on top of a large baking sheet and set aside.

Cut the pork into 2-inch (5 cm) cubes. In a medium bowl, combine the flour, salt and cumin. Add the pork and toss until evenly coated.

In a large Dutch oven, heat 3 tablespoons (45 mL) of the oil over high heat. When the oil is shimmering, add about a quarter of the pork and sear on all sides. Using tongs, remove the pork and set it on the wire rack to drain. Repeat until all of the pork has been seared.

In the same Dutch oven over high heat, add the remaining 3 tablespoons (45 mL) oil. Add the onion and reduce the heat to medium. Cook, stirring occasionally, until the onion softens but does not brown, about 10 minutes.

Meanwhile, remove the stems from the cilantro leaves and set aside the leaves. Trim the root ends from the stems and discard. Mince the stems and add them to the Dutch oven along with the garlic. Continue cooking for 5 minutes, stirring occasionally. Add the tomato paste and cook for 2 to 3 minutes, until the colour changes from fire engine red to brick red. Add the tomatoes and use a potato masher to break them down a bit. Give the empty tomato can a quick run under the tap to get every last bit of tomato out and splash that liquid into the Dutch oven. Add the stock and 1 chipotle pepper (or 2 if you are brave) and all of the adobo sauce from the can.

continues

Return the pork to the Dutch oven. Increase the heat to high and bring to a boil. Reduce the heat to low and simmer gently for 2 hours, until the pork is fork tender. Roughly chop the cilantro leaves and sprinkle on top of the adobo. Serve hot over rice with lime wedges.

Store the adobo in an airtight container in the fridge for up to 5 days or freeze in zip-top bags for up to 3 months.

TIP: If you can get your hands on some pig's feet, throw one or two in the adobo along with the seared pork shoulder or butt. In my house, we eat few traditional cuts (rib-eye, loin, etc.) because I try to buy the best possible quality meat from local farmers who practise sustainable or regenerative farming, and those cuts are too expensive for my everyday budget. I would rather eat less meat, less often and pay more to ensure that it is coming from a source I trust. Using good bones and cuts with connective tissue and collagen, such as pig's feet, gives you better flavour, more nutrition and a richer, thicker sauce.

THREE-ALARM TURKEY CHILI

Serves 8 to 10

[C] Turkey Chili is by no means traditional, but there's something really wonderful and hearty about this stew. It can be eaten very simply, straight out of the pot, or dressed up a bit with avocado and other garnishes. If you are cooking just for adults, you can add an additional 1 teaspoon (5 mL), or more, of chili powder (remember, you can always add, but you can't take away!), but if you're serving this to young people, I recommend keeping a bottle of hot sauce handy for yourself and keeping the spice level as suggested below, or even reducing it by half.

2 tablespoons (30 mL) olive oil

1 pound (450 g) ground turkey

1 tablespoon (15 mL) chili powder

1 tablespoon (15 mL) kosher salt

1 teaspoon (5 mL) dried oregano

1 teaspoon (5 mL) ground cumin

1 medium onion, diced (about
1½ cups/375 mL)

2 cloves garlic, minced

2 tablespoons (30 mL) tomato
paste

2 cans (14 ounces/400 g each)
diced tomatoes

1 can (15 ounces/425 mL) pinto
beans

1 can (15 ounces/425 mL) red
kidney beans

FOR SERVING

Full-fat sour cream

Diced avocado

Chopped cilantro

Shredded cheddar or Monterey
Jack cheese

In a large Dutch oven, heat the olive oil over medium-high heat. Add the turkey, chili powder, salt, oregano and cumin. Brown the meat, making sure to break up any large chunks and stirring occasionally to coat the meat evenly with the seasoning. Add the onion and reduce the heat to medium. Cook for about 5 minutes, or until the onion is translucent. Add the garlic and continue cooking for 1 to 2 minutes. Add the tomato paste and cook, stirring continuously, for an additional 1 to 2 minutes. Add the tomatoes and reduce the heat to medium-low. Cover and let simmer for 15 minutes. Add the pinto beans and kidney beans. Cover and continue cooking for 10 minutes.

Serve the chili hot with a dollop of sour cream, a few chunks of avocado and a sprinkling each of cilantro and cheese on top. Store leftovers in an airtight container in the fridge for up to 5 days or freeze in zip-top bags for up to 3 months.

TIP: Some recipes in other cookbooks will advise you to add the onions and garlic at the same time. Because onions are usually diced large and garlic is minced, I like to cook the onion a bit first, so that it has more time to soften and the garlic doesn't burn.

THREE'S COMPANY

[C] My womb, it turns out, is a hospitable place. It had never occurred to me that I wouldn't give birth early. Forty weeks is the norm for gestating one human, sure, but carrying twins past thirty-four or thirty-six weeks is unusual.

After twenty weeks, I had packed my bags. I was convinced I would go into labour at any moment and was secretly hoping I could get out of some of my pre–maternity leave to-do list at work. I had watched enough sitcom pregnancies that I was prepared for my water to break at an inopportune moment and to be rapidly wheeled through the hospital by a handsome Patrick Dempsey type who was efficient but concerned, quick-footed and pithy.

That never happened. Instead, at thirty-six weeks, while I was still working, I took the morning off for yet another OB-GYN visit. "Please," I begged Dr. B, exhausted and bleary eyed, "just get them out of me. They are ready. I promise."

My induction was scheduled for two weeks later. I suppose Dr. B still wanted to give them a chance to make their own way into the world. Like their mama, they were stubborn.

And so, it wasn't sitcom-y at all. I ate a slice of pizza and calmly took an Uber to the hospital. Then, I waited. And waited some more. After two hours or so, I handed over my credit card and was properly checked in and put in a fancy maternity room. The gown I was given just barely reached around my stomach, which had long ago ceased to register kicks or hiccups because space was at a premium. I took the only pregnancy selfie I have. I revelled in the free cable and spent hours watching Guy Fieri.

Eventually things sped up. My water was broken for me. I was hooked up to an IV. I wasn't sure if I was going to get an epidural because I didn't really know what to expect, pain-wise. Once they induced me by pumping me with Pitocin, I was suddenly very sure. The anesthesiologist was summoned, and I leaned into a nurse, who more or less held me in a headlock (nicely!), while the epidural was administered. Something that felt like mercury, cool and numbing, flowed through my lower limbs. I ate a popsicle and went to sleep.

While I slept, nurses came and went, periodically waking me up by prodding my cervix. I'd had a lonely pregnancy, and these motherly women, with their sensible shoes and stern but kind demeanour, were deeply comforting. For the first time in a long time, I felt that people were looking after me and that I wasn't a burden or, worse, an embarrassment. I was there to do something important.

Finally, it was time. Still feeling nothing, but not *nothing*, from the waist down, I was wheeled into the operating room. Because multiple births often require a C-section, all pretense of it being a regular birth is abandoned from the get-go. You start in the OR so the nurses don't have to sprint you there at the last minute.

I'd met the delivery doctor only briefly before. He had a small team. Some random playlist was on, but of course I'd never bothered with a birth plan, let alone programmed a birthing playlist, so I just gritted my teeth, grabbed the backs of my thighs and bore down to the musical stylings of Harry Styles. I had assumed things would go sideways at some point, and after I delivered one baby with a strange, almost removed, burst of pressure, they did. Well, she did.

Folklore says that the second twin is always the dominant one. Twin B pushes Twin A out to check and see if the coast is clear. Although Piper came out with relative ease, Matilda clearly missed the signal that all was safe. The team of people around me suddenly grew, and though I often miss social cues, there was no mistaking that after several minutes of pushing we weren't exactly in a good spot when the doctor called for the anesthesiologist again.

As everyone scurried around at their tasks and the playlist boomed around me (it had degraded to Nickelback, which I truly regret not asking them to mute), I shut out everything but my own strength and pushed.

Matilda somersaulted out of me. Sideways. But she had arrived at last. Two babies: 6 pounds, 9 ounces and 6 pounds, 2 ounces. I had delivered almost 13 pounds of baby.

In seven minutes, I went from being an individual to a duo to a family. That took some time to sink in. But as I stared at these two people I'd been growing for thirty-eight weeks, who moments ago had been living inside me, I knew that everything had changed and that our adventure had just begun.

BROTHY WHITE BEANS AND GREENS

Serves 4 to 6

[C] I don't have a nonna, but if I did, I like to imagine I would have stolen this recipe from her (and tweaked it!). The humble bean is at the centre of this dish, but in my opinion, dark leafy greens and a squeeze of lemon are what make a very plain dish something special.

1 cup (250 mL) dried white beans, such as cannellini

2 tablespoons (30 mL) olive oil

3 mild Italian sausages

1 medium onion, thinly sliced

Small handful of fresh thyme

3 bay leaves

4 cups (1 L) chicken or vegetable stock

4 to 5 cups (1 to 1.25 L) chopped broccoli rabe, chard, collards or kale

Zest and juice of 1 lemon

Salt and pepper

FOR SERVING

Extra-virgin olive oil

Freshly grated Pecorino Romano cheese

Toasted sourdough bread

TIP: Save the rinds from Pecorino Romano and Parmesan cheese in a zip-top bag in the freezer. They are great for adding a bit of oomph to pasta sauces and brothy dishes like this one. Just drop a rind or two in when you add the broth, cook the beans as usual and remove the rinds before serving.

In a medium bowl, soak the beans overnight in about 4 to 5 cups (1 to 1.25 L) cold water. If you don't have time for that, you can do a quick soak: place the beans in a medium saucepan, cover with 4 to 5 cups (1 to 1.25 L) water and bring to a boil. Turn off the heat immediately. Let the beans soak for 1 hour.

In a large Dutch oven, heat the olive oil over medium heat. Add the sausages and cook, turning occasionally, until they are browned evenly, about 5 to 7 minutes. Reduce the heat to medium and add the onion. Cook, stirring occasionally, for 7 to 10 minutes, or until the onions are soft.

Remove the sausages from the Dutch oven and place them on a clean cutting board. Cut each sausage in half, length-wise, and chop into ¾-inch (2 cm) pieces. Transfer the sausage to a plate and put it in the fridge.

Drain and rinse the beans, then add them to the Dutch oven with the onions. Tie the thyme and bay leaves together with a piece of kitchen twine and drop the bundle in the Dutch oven. Pour in the stock. Increase the heat to high and bring to a boil, then reduce the heat to medium-low and let simmer, covered, for 1 to 1¼ hours, until the beans are tender. Return the sausage to the Dutch oven. Add the broccoli rabe and stir briefly, until the greens are wilted. Turn off the heat. Season with the lemon zest and juice and the salt and pepper, to taste.

Serve hot with a drizzle of olive oil and a generous amount of Pecorino on top and a thick-cut piece of toasted sourdough on the side. Store leftovers in an airtight container in the fridge for up to 5 days or freeze in zip-top bags for up to 3 months.

FAIRY GODMOTHER MINESTRONE

Serves 4 to 6, with leftovers

[E] On the day I was born, my parents' next-door neighbour, Gail White, was making minestrone. When my parents arrived home from the hospital, she greeted them with her warming, hearty vegetable soup. Nearly thirty years later, on the night after Ezzie was born, she brought over a pot of her minestrone with some crusty sourdough and a big hunk of Parmesan. We dimmed the lights, opened some red wine and had a picnic. The way the recipe is written, it's more stew than soup, which is how I like it, but feel free to add more stock or go a bit lighter on the vegetables if you prefer more liquid. If you're making it to freeze, leave out the pasta, green beans and peas and add them when you're ready to serve.

3 tablespoons (45 mL) olive oil

3 cloves garlic, minced

1 large yellow onion, chopped

3 stalks celery, chopped

3 medium carrots, chopped

½ small head green cabbage, chopped

½ head cauliflower, cut into small florets

1 head endive or escarole, chopped

1 sprig fresh rosemary

Large handful of fresh basil leaves, chopped

Large handful of fresh parsley leaves, chopped

1 jar (24 ounces/680 mL) Italian strained tomatoes

2 to 3 rinds Parmesan or Pecorino Romano cheese (optional)

1 can (14 ounces/400 mL) navy beans, drained and rinsed (optional)

2 cups (500 mL) vegetable stock or water

Salt and pepper

In a large stockpot, heat the olive oil over medium heat until it begins to shimmer. Add the garlic, onion, celery and carrots. Cook, stirring regularly with a wooden spoon, until fragrant but not browned, about 3 minutes. Add the cabbage, cauliflower, endive, rosemary, basil and parsley. Cook, stirring occasionally, for 5 to 10 minutes, or until the vegetables begin to soften. Cover and cook for another 10 to 15 minutes, until tender. Add the strained tomatoes, cheese rinds (if using), navy beans (if using) and stock. Stir to combine, bring to a boil and then reduce to a simmer and cook with the lid askew for another 20 minutes. Season with salt and pepper, to taste. If you're making the minestrone to freeze, remove the pot from the heat, let cool to room temperature, fish out and discard the rosemary sprig and cheese rinds (if using) and freeze in a 1-gallon (4L) zip-top bag for up to 3 months.

When ready to serve, cook the pasta in a large pot of salted, boiling water according to package instructions, less 2 minutes. Drain the pasta and add it with the green beans and peas to the simmering pot of minestrone. Once the beans and peas are tender, remove the pot from the heat.

To serve, divide the minestrone among soup bowls and toss 2 to 3 torn-up basil leaves into each bowl. Stir a spoonful of pesto into each bowl, top with grated Parmesan and serve with crusty bread. Store leftovers in an airtight container in the fridge for up to 5 days.

FOR SERVING

1 cup (250 mL) small shell pasta or
  soup pasta of choice

Handful of green beans, trimmed
  and cut in half crosswise

½ cup (125 mL) fresh or frozen
  peas

Fresh basil leaves, torn

Pesto Change-O (page 262)

Freshly grated Parmesan or
  Pecorino Romano cheese

Crusty bread

POLISH MEATBALLS WITH LEMON AND CARAWAY

Serves 5 to 6

[C] I am passionate about cabbage rolls, but I'm also passionate about efficiency (remember, I have twins!) and I could never be bothered to make filling, steam cabbage leaves, hand-pack the fillings into the leaves and braise them. Necessity is the mother of invention, and this recipe is effectively a deconstructed cabbage roll. Same big flavours, same amazing partner for pierogies and sour cream, just a LOT less work.

1 tablespoon (15 ml) olive oil

3 bay leaves

1 tablespoon (15 mL) fennel seeds

2 cans (28 ounces/800 g each) whole tomatoes, plus 1 can of water

2 pounds (900 g) ground pork

1 pound (450 g) ground beef

1 cup (250 mL) cooked long grain rice

1 egg, beaten

1 tablespoon (15 mL) kosher salt, more for seasoning

1 teaspoon (5 mL) black pepper, more for seasoning

1 teaspoon (5 mL) sweet Spanish paprika

2 teaspoons (10 mL) dried dill

FOR SERVING

1½ pounds (675 g) pierogies

1 head green cabbage, cut into 5 or 6 wedges

Full-fat sour cream

Caraway seeds

Lemon wedges, for squeezing

In a large Dutch oven, heat the olive oil over medium-high heat. Add the bay leaves and fennel seeds and cook until fragrant and sizzling, about 3 to 4 minutes. Add the tomatoes. Using a potato masher, mash the tomatoes until they break down a bit but are still chunky. Add the water and stir to combine. Place the Dutch oven over medium-high heat and bring to a simmer.

Meanwhile, in a large bowl, combine the pork, beef, rice, egg, salt, pepper, paprika and dill. Knead together and, working quickly, roll into balls somewhere between the size of a golf ball and a tennis ball. (The size of the meatballs depends on personal preference. I like a larger ball, but should you prefer a smaller ball, have at it and reduce the cooking time.)

Gently drop the meatballs into the tomato mixture. Cover and simmer over medium-low heat for 25 to 30 minutes, until cooked through. Fish out the bay leaves and discard. Using a slotted spoon, transfer the meatballs to a clean plate. Increase heat to medium and cook the sauce for 10 to 15 minutes, stirring occasionally, until thickened. Return the meatballs to the pot. Season with salt and pepper, to taste.

Meanwhile, bring a large pot of salted water to a boil. Cook the pierogies according to package instructions and set aside. In the same water, boil the cabbage wedges for 6 to 8 minutes, until tender.

Serve the meatballs with the boiled cabbage and pierogies. Top with sour cream, caraway seeds and lemon juice. Store leftover meatballs in an airtight container in the fridge for up to 5 days or freeze in zip-top bags for up to 3 months.

RED PEPPER CURRY CHICKEN

Serves 4

[C] My father always referred to himself as "the chef" and to my mom as "the cook." He rarely used cookbooks and often cooked on the edge (precipice, really) of his skill and knowledge. The one cookbook that he did tatter and splatter with use was Madhur Jaffrey's *Indian Cookery*. Jaffrey is an institution in Indian cooking, and this recipe is a riff on her Lal Masale Wali Murghi, which for me still represents the taste of my childhood.

CURRY SAUCE

½ cup (125 mL) water

4 large red bell peppers, seeded and chopped

1-inch (2.5 cm) piece fresh ginger, peeled

3 cloves garlic, smashed

Handful of fresh cilantro stems

¼ cup (60 mL) cashew butter

1 tablespoon (15 mL) ground cumin

1 tablespoon (15 mL) ground coriander seeds

1 teaspoon (5 mL) turmeric

1 to 2 red bird's eye chilies, to taste

1 tablespoon (15 mL) salt

CHICKEN

1 whole chicken, about 2 to 3 pounds (1 to 1.35 kg)

Salt and pepper

¼ cup (60 mL) olive oil or ghee

FOR SERVING

Cooked long grain rice

Fresh cilantro leaves

Lemon wedges

To make the curry sauce, place all of the ingredients in a high-speed blender. Purée on high until smooth. If you want to save the sauce to use later, freeze it in a zip-top bag for up to 3 months.

To make the chicken, use a sharp knife to remove the legs and breasts from the chicken. If you've never done this before, remember that you are a capable adult and that YouTube has a video tutorial for everything. You may not get it perfect the first time, but that's okay—no one will notice, and we all start somewhere. Pop the chicken carcass into a zip-top bag and freeze it for when you make Chicken Stock (page 255) in the future. Season the chicken pieces liberally with salt and pepper.

In a skillet, heat the olive oil over medium-high heat. Once it begins to shimmer, add the chicken and brown for about 2 minutes on each side. Transfer the chicken to a clean plate and set aside.

To the same olive oil, add the sauce. Cook for 5 minutes, stirring occasionally, until it reduces slightly. Add the chicken to the sauce and cook for 20 to 30 minutes, until the chicken is cooked through. If you're not sure, you can do what I always do and poke a paring knife into the thickest part of the breast to see if it is opaque and cooked; or, if you have a thermometer, you want it to read 165°F (75°C).

Serve the chicken and sauce over rice. Garnish each portion with cilantro and a wedge of lemon. Store the chicken in an airtight container in the fridge for up to 5 days or freeze in zip-top bags for up to 3 months.

TIP: This recipe is easily doubled or even quadrupled. If you're making it for little-people palates, ease off on the chilies, but don't be shy about serving it because this is a great recipe to introduce children to complex flavours. If you're concerned about the spice level, thin the sauce by stirring in half or even a whole can (14 ounces/400 mL) of coconut milk just before serving. Serve with extra rice.

SOUR CREAM SCONES

Makes 8 scones

[E] This recipe, adapted from a neatly printed card in my mom's recipe box, is for the fluffy, not-too-sweet scones she makes once a year on Christmas morning. As kids, my sister and I thought they were called *swans*, which added to their mystique. If you keep a stash of raw dough in your freezer, you can have Christmas morning in your jammies anytime you feel like it—one of the many perks of motherhood.

2 cups (500 mL) all-purpose flour
4 tablespoons (60 mL) granulated
　sugar, divided
½ teaspoon (2 mL) baking soda
2 teaspoons (10 mL) baking
　powder
½ teaspoon (2 mL) salt
5 tablespoons (75 mL) cold
　unsalted butter
1 egg
1¼ cups (300 mL) full-fat sour
　cream

FOR SERVING
Unsalted butter
Clotted cream
Raspberry Chia Jam (page 257)
Lemon Curd (page 259)

Preheat the oven to 400°F (200°C).

In a medium bowl, sift together the flour, 2 tablespoons (30 mL) of the sugar, baking soda, baking powder and salt. Using a box grater, grate in the butter.

In a small bowl, lightly beat the egg. Add the egg and sour cream to the dry ingredients. Using a wooden spoon, stir until just combined.

Onto a large clean surface, such as a cutting board or countertop, sprinkle a thin layer of flour. Flour your hands and transfer the dough to the lightly floured surface. Knead for 10 seconds, until the shaggy, sticky dough just comes together. Divide the dough into 2 equal mounds. Using a sharp knife, score each into quarters and sprinkle each mound with about 1 tablespoon (15 mL) sugar. If you're making the scones ahead to freeze, rather than merely scoring the dough balls, cut each one all the way through into quarters. Individual scones will bake more evenly from frozen. Freeze individually on a parchment-lined baking sheet for 15 minutes and then transfer to a zip-top bag and freeze for up to 3 months.

Bake from room temperature or frozen for 20 to 22 minutes, or until lightly brown on top and the inside is fluffy, not doughy (peek in along the score marks). Break into 8 scones (if not baking from frozen) and serve hot with butter, clotted cream, Raspberry Chia Jam and/or Lemon Curd.

CHOCOLATE CHIP BANANA CAKE

Makes 1 (9- × 13-inch/3.5 L) pan cake

[C] This is a sort of magic cake. First, because there's an alchemy that happens between bananas and chocolate when they hang out together and, second, because it never seems to totally freeze and when you have a "hangry" sweet tooth, you can eat it right out of the freezer, which I did regularly both pre- and postpartum.

2 cups (500 mL) all-purpose flour

2 teaspoons (10 mL) baking powder

1 teaspoon (5 mL) baking soda

Pinch of salt

½ cup (125 mL) unsalted butter, softened

1½ cups (375 mL) granulated sugar

2 large or 3 medium ripe bananas

3 eggs

1 teaspoon (5 mL) pure vanilla extract

½ cup (125 mL) full-fat plain yogurt or full-fat sour cream, divided

1 cup (250 mL) dark chocolate chips

Preheat the oven to 350°F (180°C). Lightly grease a 9- × 13-inch (3.5 L) baking dish with non-stick cooking spray.

In a large bowl, sift together the flour, baking powder, baking soda and salt.

In a medium bowl, cream the butter and sugar, until they are≈light and fluffy.

In a high-speed blender or food processor, add the bananas, eggs and vanilla and purée until smooth. Pour the banana mixture into the butter and sugar mixture and stir with a rubber spatula until fully combined.

Add about a third of the dry ingredients to the wet ingredients. Using a rubber spatula, fold in the dry ingredients until just combined. Add ¼ cup (60 mL) of the yogurt and fold until just combined. Repeat. Add the final third of the flour and the chocolate chips. Fold to combine, making sure no pockets of flour remain.

Transfer the batter to the prepared baking dish and spread it in an even layer. Bake for 40 to 50 minutes, or until a toothpick inserted into the centre of the cake comes out clean and the sides of the cake start to pull away from the baking dish. Let cool slightly in the baking dish before serving.

Store the cake in an airtight container in the fridge for up to 5 days or freeze, quartered and wrapped tightly in plastic wrap, for up to 3 months.

DELIVERANCE

[E] They say women forget the pain of childbirth almost immediately after it's over. That seemed risky to me, so two days after giving birth, I recorded the events in as much detail as I could summon. The following is written in the present tense so you can feel present (and tense).

Thursday, January 25, 2018, 1:30 AM

We just got home from the office and into our pyjamas. Anthony is still emailing. I feel a bit strange. Maybe it was the four-cheese rigatoni.

Saturday is the due date, but I have every reason to believe the baby will be late. Most first babies are late. Also, our company is raising money for the first time and I am not feeling relaxed or motherly. If I were Ezzie (her real name will be Esmé, but we mostly think of her as Ezzie), I wouldn't be in any rush.

I had a few twinges at the office on Monday night, which prompted me to start emailing my passwords around in a rather dramatic fashion (Tom, our friend and finance guy, looked up and asked, "Are you dying?"), but I've felt fine since then.

We had an early dinner out with Anthony's parents. We had pasta and very good red wine. Everyone agreed the baby would be at least a week late. Then we went back to the office.

I still feel crampy and nauseous. I think I'm going to see how my pregnancy books end, just in case.

1:50 AM

Yup, that was definitely a contraction. This is really happening.

2 AM

Anthony has downloaded a contraction-timing app.

"It's starting!" I shout from the bathroom (where it feels safest to sequester myself for the time being). The pain steepens and falls away. We repeat this over and over. We've been told to call the midwives once my contractions are at "4-1-1": every four minutes, lasting a minute, for a full hour. Anthony is in and out of a light sleep, pressing record and stop. I stay close to the toilet; I feel like I'm going to be sick, and once or twice, I am.

The peaks of pain get higher, sharper, more godawful. At one point I draw a warm bath and lie in it, which makes the searing pain in my lower back feel better. I nod off. Even though the bath is shallow and I am shaped like a flotation device, I understand through my pain haze that this is dangerous. When a break feels long enough, I get myself into bed beside Anthony and curl up on my heating pad.

5 AM

I'm lying on the bathroom floor. Anthony announces that we're at 4-1-1. We call Houley. I've been told that midwives don't come right away when you page them, especially if it's your first. Houley says she's on her way.

My midwives work in a team of three. In the early days, I wasn't sure I wanted Houley to be the one on call when I went into labour. She seemed too relaxed. By my last appointment, I had changed my mind. Hers is the calm of one who knows exactly what she's doing.

5:30 AM

Houley is here, thank God. My contractions are about three minutes apart, but it feels like ten seconds. When one is washing over me, Houley says, in her reassuring voice, *"I know."* I believe her.

She puts some kind of homeopathic sugar pill under my tongue. I ask for another and she says I can have it in 15 minutes.

5:45 AM

Another sugar pill—yes! Houley examines me and says that I am three centimetres dilated and ninety percent effaced. This is apparently good news. She asks if I'd like to go to the hospital now. I look at her like she's lost it.

Two hockey bags stuffed with pillows, books, towels, toiletries, clothes and snacks are sitting in the hall. It looks like I am going away to summer camp.

I have been planning to go to the hospital for the grand finale. I am aware that midwives come prepared for a home birth even if you're not planning for one, but the idea has never appealed to me. I like the security of a hospital, with its surgeons and apparatus and epidurals. I do not want to assume that everything will be fine. Nor do I want anything gross to happen in my nice, clean bedroom. Now all I can think is, *She wants me to go down two flights of stairs and into a CAR?*

6:45 AM

Geraldine, our doula, arrives as the sunrise becomes visible through our slanted bedroom windows, pink and orange. I'm in bed. Houley says it's time to go to the hospital—now.

I shake my head.

Houley tells me she'd like to bring her kit up from the car, just in case. I picture rubber sheets and scalpels on a tray. I'm hit with another contraction and grit my teeth. I find Houley's eyes and ask her to tell me if there is any reason to be concerned about delivering this baby at home.

"No," she says, and I believe her.

7 AM

Geraldine helps me into a warm bath to ease the pain. Ezzie is awake. My stomach heaves as she pushes her limbs against the walls of my insides, presumably looking for the neon exit sign.

The "transition" comes as I am settling into the tub. That's when what you thought was a ten on the pain scale turns out to have hardly been a two. I close my eyes and keep them closed. For some reason, I try not to swear (I'm not a Scientologist). I make guttural noises. A Mozart symphony is playing, apparently at my request. I demand that it be silenced. Miles Davis plays. I let him go on.

9 or so AM

I hear the backup midwife arrive with a student and apologize to them for not being able to introduce myself properly just now. It's an odd thing to say when I'm naked in a tub surrounded by kneeling people in clothes, but my eyes are still closed, so I don't notice. "That's okay," the student offers.

Who the f*#$ knows AM

The team kneeling around me tells me to push. My water breaks, finally. I scream and swear with gusto. Feeling like death is imminent, I tell Geraldine, "I CAN'T DO THIS." Then, using all my strength, with one final push it feels like my body is coming apart. And she is beside me in the water.

10:13 AM

I open my eyes.

She stays underwater for a moment or two. Having come from amniotic fluid, she still gets her oxygen from the umbilical cord. Houley lifts her out, and her little body turns pink as she takes her very first gulp of air. She starts to cry.

Then Houley puts her on my chest. She feels soft and real. She brings me back into the world.

Saturday, January 27, 2018 (my due date), 6 PM

I'm propped up in our bed with a sleeping face smooshed into my chest, bow-shaped lips crumpled against my skin. She's hugging me with her tiny arms like a tree frog. It was "back labour," and she was facing the wrong way until the last minute, I later learned. "Sunny side up," they call it. I remember very clearly that it hurt like hell. But I would do it again.

LABOUR DAY LEMONADE

Makes 4 cups (1 L)

[E] I drank this concoction during labour on the advice of my naturopath, Christina Gordon.

Juice of 1 lemon
1 tablespoon (15 mL) maple syrup
1 tablespoon (15 mL) unflavoured
   magnesium powder
4 cups (1 L) filtered water

In a large pitcher or reusable bottle, stir or shake the lemon juice, maple syrup and magnesium powder into the water. Make ahead of time to have on hand on game day.

ONE HAND, ONE LOVE

The part when you're hungrier than ever and always holding a baby (at least one).

[E] Babies are hungry-making creatures. In the first few months postpartum, I devoured seconds and thirds of everything within reach of my baby-free arm. Thankfully, everyone brought food. My dad baked 2 AM Cookies (page 158), my mom and mother-in-law kept me in crudités, cheese and olives, my sister and siblings-in-law filled the kitchen with magical smells, my stepmom brought party sandwiches and my father-in-law brought crispy shrimp rolls and wonton soup (a long-standing Sunday tradition).

And Christine. Boy, did she put my pierogies to shame, quietly depositing many home-made delights on our doorstep. All of these gifts, beyond providing welcome energy, gave me another form of sustenance, too. The quiet recognition that I was doing something hard and needed the support of my people at that moment. If only all new mothers could be so lucky.

[C] This book is called *How to Eat with One Hand*, but we never promised to teach you how to cook with one hand. That's because you'll need help, whether it's from a partner, a mother(-in-law), a father(-in-law) or a friend. So this chapter is a mix of things you can make on your own, such as Golden Milk Chia Pudding (page 107), Pan con Tomate (page 122) and Green Pepper Pot Soup (page 129), and of recipes to dog-ear for other people to make for you.

Everything, of course, can be eaten with minimal cutlery, but this chapter is important because it asks you to lean on other people, and we know that can be hard. Being a new mom is isolating. You are simultaneously very needed and very alone, especially if you are on your own or your partner is at work. There are long, long hours of podcasts and Netflix and feeding. So, Emma and I are here to remind you to ask for a bit of help and a bit of company now and again. When people ask, "Can I bring you anything?" don't plaster on a chipmunk smile and say, "I'm FINE, everything is GREAT!" Instead, ask for Turkey Tetrazzini (page 147) or perhaps Cool Hand Zucc (page 108).

GOLDEN MILK CHIA PUDDING

Serves 4

[C] I like chia pudding, but there needs to be something interesting about it to keep me dipping my spoon back in there. Often it's crunchy toppings, but in this recipe the taste is so bright and fresh, I can eat it ungarnished. More complex than your basic vanilla chia pudding, this version takes its cue from golden milk lattes and includes fresh lemon to make everything feel zippy and refreshing.

1 can (14 ounces/400 mL) full-fat coconut milk

1½ cups (375 mL) water

2 tablespoons (30 mL) pure liquid honey

Zest and juice of 1 lemon

1 tablespoon (15 mL) ginger juice (optional)

2 teaspoons (10 mL) ground turmeric

Pinch of ground cinnamon

Pinch of ground nutmeg

Pinch of ground ginger

Pinch of black pepper

Pinch of salt (optional)

½ cup (125 mL) chia seeds

TOPPINGS (OPTIONAL)

Goji berries

Bee pollen

Toasted unsweetened shredded coconut

Dried or fresh golden berries

Dried mulberries

Raspberry Chia Jam (page 257)

In a medium bowl, whisk together the coconut milk, water, honey, lemon zest and juice, ginger juice (if using), turmeric, cinnamon, nutmeg, ginger, pepper and salt (if using), until combined. Whisk in the chia seeds and continue whisking for 1 to 2 minutes to break up any lumps. Cover and let set for a few hours, or overnight, in the fridge.

Before serving, whisk the chia pudding to loosen up any lumps. Divide it among 4 small bowls. Top each bowl with Goji berries, bee pollen, coconut, golden berries and/or mulberries, or use whatever speaks to you from your own fridge or pantry.

Store the chia pudding, without toppings, in an airtight container in the fridge for up to 5 days.

TIP: If the chia pudding becomes too stiff after sitting in the fridge for a few days, just whisk in 1 to 2 tablespoons (15 to 30 mL) of water to loosen it.

COOL HAND ZUCC

Makes 1 (9- × 5-inch/2 L) loaf

[C] During my pregnancy, I had deadlines that needed to be met if I wanted to take a maternity leave—notably, developing new baked goods for our restaurant group. My business partner, Alan, tasked me with making a delicious snack loaf—sweet but not too sweet, no conventional flours, lots of seeds, a pithy name—and I spent months researching, tweaking and testing before handing the recipe over to the restaurant teams on more or less my last day of work. I got the recipe in on time, but in order to vet a recipe we also do taste tests and then make small corrections or clarify instructions. The turnaround on that is usually another 1 to 2 weeks. A few hours or so after giving birth twice, I found myself groggily accepting zucchini loaf samples from each of our restaurants to taste and review. I have a soft spot for this loaf for a few reasons, but more than that, I just think it tastes really good before, after or, let's face it, during delivery.

2 cups (500 mL) grated zucchini

1 cup (250 mL) pure maple syrup

¾ cup (175 mL) dairy or nut milk of choice

½ cup (125 mL) virgin coconut oil, melted

2 tablespoons (30 mL) chia seeds

1 tablespoon (15 mL) apple cider vinegar

2½ cups (625 mL) spelt flour

1 tablespoon (15 mL) baking powder

1 teaspoon (5 mL) baking soda

1 teaspoon (5 mL) cinnamon

1 teaspoon (5 mL) salt

¾ cup (175 mL) rolled oats

1 cup (500 mL) roughly chopped dried mission figs

¼ cup (60 mL) pumpkin seeds

¼ cup (60 mL) sunflower seeds

¼ cup (60 mL) millet

2 tablespoons (30 mL) unsweetened shredded coconut

Preheat the oven to 375°F (190°C). Lightly grease a 9- × 5-inch (2 L) loaf pan with non-stick cooking spray.

In a medium bowl, stir together the zucchini, maple syrup, milk, coconut oil, chia seeds and vinegar.

In a large bowl, sift together the spelt flour, baking powder, baking soda, cinnamon and salt. Add the oats, figs, pumpkin and sunflower seeds, millet and coconut. Pour the wet ingredients into the dry ingredients and, using a rubber spatula, stir until just combined.

Transfer the batter to the prepared loaf pan. Bake for 70 minutes, or until the loaf is golden and firm to the touch and the sides of the loaf start to pull away from the pan. Let cool in the pan for 10 minutes before transferring the loaf to a wire rack to cool completely.

Store the loaf in a zip-top bag in the fridge for up to 5 days or wrap tightly with plastic wrap and freeze for up to 3 months.

TIP: This loaf is pretty forgiving, so if you want to use raisins instead of figs or swap out the sunflower seeds for walnuts, go for it—just be sure to use equal amounts.

PEANUT BUTTER MOTHER LOVER

Serves 1

[C] I did my best to breastfeed two babies, but it was hard for a number of reasons. For the first couple of weeks I was pumping or breastfeeding at least 13 hours a day, and it never seemed like enough milk was coming out of me or enough food was going in. Drinkable calories—for the first time in my life—were a good thing. This recipe is delicious, requires no real planning and, I'll be honest, if you throw in a splash of Baileys, it doesn't hurt.

2 Medjool dates, pitted

1 large banana

2 heaping teaspoons (12 mL) cacao powder

2 heaping tablespoons (36 mL) natural peanut butter

½ cup (125 mL) Vanilla Almond Milk (page 20) or nut milk of choice

Pinch of salt

1 cup (250 mL) ice cubes

Place the dates in a small bowl of warm water and let soak for 10 minutes, until softened. If you don't have time for this step, just chop them up a bit.

Place the dates, banana, cacao, peanut butter, milk and salt in a blender. Add the ice. Blend for 30 to 45 seconds, or until smooth. Serve immediately.

TIP: Anytime you are making a smoothie, add the ice last. The ice will press down the other ingredients, which will help them blend, and since the ice blends last, your smoothie will come out colder and a little thicker.

MORINGA MATCHA

Makes 1 cup (250 mL)

[E] My sister-in-law Deeva turned me on to moringa, a nutrient-dense tree that has long been prized for its health benefits. High in protein, vitamins, folate, calcium and iron, moringa leaf powder is known as "mother's best friend" because of its reputation for increasing milk supply in nursing mothers. Even if it doesn't do that for you (or you don't need it for that), moringa powder is a helpful way to get some extra nutrients into your morning matcha or smoothie. A word of warning: moringa leaf powder has a very grassy taste; start with a small dose and use a high-fat milk like homemade nut milk, coconut milk or whole milk for this latte.

1 cup (250 mL) Vanilla Almond Milk (page 20) or milk of choice

½ teaspoon (2 mL) matcha powder

¼ to ½ teaspoon (1 to 2 mL) moringa leaf powder

½ teaspoon (2 mL) pure maple syrup or honey, or to taste

In a small saucepan over medium heat, warm up the milk.

In a small bowl or the mug you plan to drink from, combine the matcha and moringa powders. Add about a quarter of the warm milk and whisk until well mixed and frothy. Top with the remaining warm milk and sweeten with the maple syrup or honey. Stir to combine and serve warm.

CINNAMON HOCHO

Makes 1 cup (250 mL)

[E] Motherhood can be pretty stressful. You might find yourself needing a hot chocolate from time to time, to take the edge off. This one is rich, warming and not too sweet.

1 cup (250 mL) Vanilla Almond Milk (page 20) or milk of choice

1 tablespoon (15 mL) cocoa powder

¼ teaspoon (1 mL) ground cinnamon

¼ teaspoon (1 mL) pure vanilla extract

1 tablespoon (15 mL) pure maple syrup, or to taste

In a small saucepan over medium heat, warm up the milk.

In a small bowl or the mug you plan to drink from, combine the cocoa and cinnamon. Add about a quarter of the warm milk and whisk until well mixed and frothy. Top with the remaining warm milk, add the vanilla and sweeten with the maple syrup. Stir to combine and serve warm.

BREASTFEEDING: IT'S COMPLICATED

[E] One of the many things I did not know before becoming a mother was how immersive breastfeeding would be.

"You didn't?" my mom exclaimed when I told her this. "You should have asked me."

My mother-in-law Denyse had warned me that breastfeeding can be painful, but I hadn't asked enough follow-up questions. What she meant was not just that your nipples will hurt—of course they will—and that the skin might break, which is like when you get a blister and have to keep walking in those shoes. She also meant that the first few feeds will feel like childbirth all over again. Breastfeeding sends hormones through your body that tell the uterus, now an empty room, to contract. I remember breathing through my teeth and thinking that it sounded like tiny people were moving furniture in my abdomen.

I also failed to realize that while the baby is learning to latch, breastfeeding is a full-time job. The morning of my daughter's birth, my midwife gave me a form to fill in with feeds and outputs. I timed every feed at first, until I saw that my daughter was at the breast for twelve hours a day and decided it would be healthier not to keep track.

Once I got my hands on some Advil and a jar of prescription nipple cream, though, it wasn't so bad. Trying to manoeuvre my daughter's head into a position that would help her latch ("big mouth, Ezzie" was my sister-in-law Sophie's gentle refrain), configuring pillows to avoid tennis elbow and eating like an Olympic swimmer were my primary occupations. Several times a day I drank a hot, honey-laced tea made from herbs that are meant to stimulate milk production (you can find it at the health food store).

I was lucky: Ezzie was latching well. Three days after her birth, my milk "came in." That night, I lay awake in a cold sweat with Ezzie on my chest and the bed stripped of blankets and pillows, convinced that something terrible would happen if Anthony or I fell asleep. It took me a few days to realize that my shifting hormones might have had something to do with these waves of anxiety.

[C] I got off to a shaky start with breastfeeding. Before checking out of the hospital, a lactation consultant came to my room. My parents were not hovering but were present, and my dad was ready to drive my daughters home in the car seats I had rented for the event. I don't remember this woman's name, but I'll never forget the horror I felt as she grabbed my very large, very swollen breast out of my nursing nightie and jammed it into my daughter's mouth. "You have a very generous breast, so it's hard for her to get her mouth around it. You've got to help her; squeeze your breast! Right now, you've got her trying to eat a hamburger sideways." My father found something interesting on the other side of the room, and I willed myself not to cry at what felt like a very personal and public criticism.

By the time I got the girls home, I was ready to give it another try, and I stuck with it through the first couple of days when it felt like nothing was coming out (really, not much was) until I finally felt something give inside me and production booted up. Relief washed through me. Still, it wasn't enough, and by our first pediatrician appointment a few days later, the girls had lost more than twelve percent of their birth weight. I felt like a failure as I scooped yellowish white powder into sterilized bottles. My generous breasts weren't so generous after all.

But the formula was a huge help: it made me more mobile and less stressed. I could escape once in a while or, as it so happened, drive two thousand kilometres without having to pull over and whip out my feeders by the side of the road in a snowstorm. What I lacked in output, however, I made up for in persistence, and I kept at it, investing in a good pump (*Why can't they make them suck harder and faster*, I bemoaned as milk trickled slowly into the tiny bottle) and slowly increasing my supply. I figured out how to do the walk-n-feed, where you position your baby carrier just low enough to get a latch so that you can actually do things while feeding. I mastered the nighttime "side-feed" (*You eat! I sleep!*). Eventually, I even gained enough confidence to attempt the most difficult feed of all, the double-feed, where you hold each baby in one arm like you're carrying a football—and yes, it's as hard as it sounds. It's what I imagine your first successful time on a unicycle must feel like. Triumphant, but aware that you could lose your balance and tumble off at any moment.

[E] My biggest breastfeeding blind spots by far were about investment and exposure. It didn't occur to me that after having been a mobile home for nine months, I might become a food truck for another eighteen. Nor had I pictured regular life resuming while breastfeeding continued. But, of course, it did, and like many French sunbathers and Hollywood stars before me, I faced the question of whether to bare the nipple.

The first time I fed Ezzie in public, it was a wintry morning and I was about to get on the streetcar. Nestled in her carrier, she went into hedgehog mode. I sat down inside the streetcar shelter, and with my parka still zipped, managed to de-layer enough to get the job done. I got a bit of a thrill from my secret multitasking. *Maybe I'll become a flasher when all of this is done*, I thought.

When the warm weather came, it was harder to be discreet. Out on a spring day, the screaming began, and I found a secluded park bench. Once I got into position, and the screaming blessedly ceased, I noticed a condom wrapper at my feet. *Well played*, I told the universe.

In the summer, at my best friend's wedding in the countryside, I spent half the party trying to nurse Ezzie to sleep behind a floor-length curtain in the living room, like Polonius or a character from the board game Clue!

I know how fortunate I was to have been able to choose whether to breastfeed, and for how long. This is often not the case. It was not the case for my mother with me, her colicky second child, and it might not be the case for me with my second child, who at the time of writing is still in utero.

At times I resented my decision, especially once I had returned to work. For six months I would come home in the evening with scalding rocks on my chest and a powerful headache building. On my return from one business trip, the two bottles of hand-pumped milk that Ezzie needed for the next day were (wrongly) confiscated at security and chucked into the trash bin, reducing me to angry tears in a corner beside Tim Hortons.

The breastfeeding question is made more complicated by the fact that everyone seems to have an opinion about it. Including a stranger standing behind me in line for the bank one day who, unprovoked (I was not flashing anyone at the time), felt the need to ask me if I was doing it, and responded to my tentative "yes…" with an infuriating, "good!" In an ideal world, no one would feel justified in passing judgement on how best to use nipples that do not belong to them.

It's none of the bank man's business, but the reason I kept breastfeeding for so long, despite the sizeable opportunity cost, was a selfish one: the final and most surprising thing I did not know about breastfeeding was that I would come to love it. The efficiency was a marvel, and the payoff—watching Ezzie fall asleep with her cheek pressed against me—was one of the many things about motherhood that would have been impossible to imagine beforehand, so it was probably for the best that I hadn't tried.

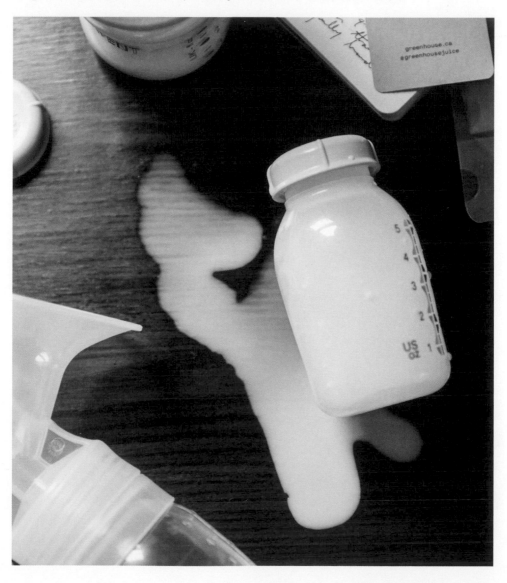

RED FLANNEL HASH

Serves 4

[C] Most foods taste better and develop more intense flavour on the day after they are cooked. Hash is a valuable culinary technique (though not a formal one), because it leverages the flavours you have already built. It's a great way to clear out your fridge and to make something warming and delicious with just a few odds and ends, a potato and about five to seven minutes of your time. The trick is to make sure your hash mix is chopped and combined well, and that the pan you put it in is smoking hot.

4 medium potatoes

4 medium beets

2 tablespoons (30 mL) unsalted butter

1 medium yellow onion, thinly sliced

1 cup (250 mL) cooked meat, such as lamb, corned beef, pulled pork or dark chicken meat (optional)

1 cup (250 mL) sauerkraut, drained

Small handful of spinach or arugula (optional)

Salt and pepper

4 tablespoons (60 mL) neutral oil, such as canola or grapeseed

4 eggs, fried or poached

FOR SERVING

½ cup (125 mL) sour cream

1 tablespoon (15 mL) caraway seeds

¼ cup (60 mL) chopped fresh parsley

Place the potatoes and beets in a large pot of salted water and bring to a boil over high heat. Cook until tender, about 20 to 25 minutes for the potatoes and 25 to 30 minutes for the beets. Use a slotted spoon to remove them from the pot when tender, then let cool in a dish before chopping into bite-size cubes.

In a large cast iron skillet, melt the butter over medium-high heat. Add the onion and reduce the heat to medium-low. Cook the onion for about 10 minutes, stirring occasionally so it doesn't brown, or until soft.

Meanwhile, in a large bowl, combine the meat (if using), potatoes, beets, sauerkraut and spinach, if using. Break up any large chunks of beet or potato to create a fairly pink and clumpy mixture. Add the onion and stir to combine. Season with salt and pepper, to taste.

Use a paper towel to wipe down the skillet you used to cook the onions. Add the oil to the skillet and heat over high heat. When the oil starts to shimmer, add the hash mix. Cook on high heat without stirring for about 5 minutes (turn it down if the oil starts to smoke). Reduce the heat to medium-low and continue cooking for about 7 to 10 minutes, until the bottom is crispy and the top is warm.

Gently place the eggs on top of the hash. Add a few dollops of sour cream and sprinkle with caraway seeds and parsley. Serve family style.

THE ELEPHANT IN THE ROOM

[C] It's me, right? The elephant, I mean. Not strictly just the idiom, although we'll talk about that in a minute.

Going into delivery, I assumed that the eighty or so pounds I'd put on would—*poof!*—disappear like some beautiful pregnancy fairy tale and I would be restored to my former, if not quite slim, then average-looking self.

Spoiler alert: I did not deliver two forty-pound babies, and even though I had rapidly expelled thirteen pounds of baby and their luggage, no instant deflation occurred.

Instead, I swelled and ballooned: my face (most alarmingly) and my feet (most annoyingly). Grossly overestimating my ability to locate my waist postpartum, I'd packed a cute midi length robe in my hospital bag. After delivering and kind of recovering, I hobbled over to the mirror. I did not like what I saw, but I pulled on my mesh surgical-grade panties and knotted the robe securely underneath my boobs and above my newly slack, but still giant belly.

It didn't stop there. My boobs kept expanding in every direction until they basically wrapped around my back. And they *hurt*. I was unbelievably proud of myself, thrilled with these magical little humans I had grown, but I also felt huge and uncomfortable and like some lumbering land mammal every time I lurched up from the low-slung couch where I spent hours breastfeeding and icing my swollen feet in a restaurant bus tub.

So, now we come to the second elephant in the room. We're offering you a book of (truly!) delicious recipes at a time when you may want to just hibernate and drink broth until you hit that first non–baby-related mother milestone: fitting into your pre-pregnancy jeans.

But here's the thing: I don't make food just because I'm hungry. I make food because I love to cook, and if you asked me for the short list of things that have kept me sane from pregnancy through surviving life with toddlers, I would say cooking.

It was hard to leave the house during those early weeks. Not emotionally. It was physically and logistically difficult. I did my best, but it took time to get the hang of how to load everyone, how far we could go and how to breastfeed in the wild.

Walking to my kitchen was easy. I'd bundle up the girls and tuck them into the corners of the couch, where I could see them from my post at the stove. They slept, I chopped. They snoozed, I sautéed. They woke up and squawked; I said, "Hold on, my loaf is almost done!" When people dropped in, I'd send them on their way with Tupperware full of soup or a slab of banana cake, and they would look at me like I was crazy—thinking I had cooked for them, when really I had cooked for myself. I felt like even though I was at the mercy of these two tiny humans and this body that I owned but that was not mine, there was still a space that I had control over, and that helped me.

In the end, thanks to a healthy ratio of spandex to denim and the absence of a button fly, my jeans fit. But that didn't happen at two weeks postpartum. Or at six weeks. It was gradual, and though I remember the feeling, I couldn't tell you the date. Because, even if elephants never forget, some things aren't worth remembering.

PAN CON TOMATE

Serves 1 to 2, depending on your mood

[C] This recipe is more than the sum of its parts. It's like the more sophisticated, more cultured cousin of avocado toast. We could have easily stuck pan con tomate, also known as "bread with tomato," into any section of this book, but we chose to put it in this section because it's a quick meal you can make for yourself, and it's easy and practical to eat, even when you are extremely busy, tired, hungry, etc. And that's how you will feel in the first couple of weeks after giving birth.

2 slices thick-cut sourdough
   bread, toasted

1 clove garlic, cut in half

1 large, ripe tomato

2 tablespoons (30 mL) extra-
   virgin olive oil

2 pinches of flakey sea salt

Lay out the toasted bread on a clean cutting board. Rub each slice with half a clove of garlic.

Cut the tomato in half crosswise. Holding the skin side firmly, use the largest holes on a box grater to grate both halves of the tomato onto a plate, applying pressure so that you end up with just the skin at the end. Discard the skin. Spoon the grated tomato evenly over the 2 slices of toast. Drizzle each slice with 1 tablespoon (15 mL) olive oil, then finish each with a pinch of flakey sea salt.

TIP: If you so choose, skip the flakey sea salt and top each slice of toast with a few small, briny tinned fish, such as anchovies or sardines. You'll feel extra Spanish, and you'll also get all kinds of calcium and healthy omega fats from the fish. *Olé!*

HIGH ACID, DEEP GREEN SALAD

Serves 4 as a side

[E] The standard ratio of acid to oil in a vinaigrette is one part acid (vinegar or lemon juice) to three parts oil. Most days, I prefer something closer to 1:2. On pregnant days, if you're like Christine and me, things might get really tart in your bowl. Building this salad in layers lets you control the bite while also ensuring even leaf coating. This recipe is inspired by my mother-in-law Denyse's classic summer salads, which often come from her garden. Add some of the optional toppings to make it a meal.

1 tablespoon (15 mL) Dijon mustard (I like Maille or Grey Poupon)

1 tablespoon (15 mL) white wine vinegar, more to taste

½ teaspoon (2 mL) flakey sea salt, more to taste

2 scallions, trimmed and thinly sliced

Handful of blanched green beans, trimmed and halved (optional)

½ cup (125 mL) blanched fresh peas (optional)

2 cups (500 mL) arugula or bitter young salad greens of choice

2 cups (500 mL) Boston or Bibb lettuce, torn into bite-size pieces

1 head endive, sliced lengthwise

2 tablespoons (30 mL) extra-virgin olive oil, more to taste

Freshly ground pepper

TOPPINGS (OPTIONAL)

Handful of toasted walnuts or sunflower seeds

2 hard-boiled eggs, peeled and sliced into halves or quarters

1 avocado, pitted, peeled and sliced

In a large salad bowl, whisk together the mustard, vinegar and salt. Add the scallions, green beans (if using) and peas (if using) and let sit for a few minutes.

Right before serving, add the arugula, lettuce and endive to the bowl 1 cup (250 mL) at a time, drizzling in ½ tablespoon (7 mL) of the olive oil after each addition of greens. Toss well to ensure that the greens are evenly coated with the oil and vinegar. Season with more vinegar, olive oil, salt and pepper, to taste. Toss to combine.

Top the dressed greens with toasted walnuts or sunflower seeds, hard-boiled eggs and/or sliced avocado, as desired.

Divide among plates or shallow bowls and serve immediately.

KABOCHA AND FETA SALAD

Serves 2 as a meal, 4 as a side

[E] Like a new mother, this salad has a lot going on. It's inspired by a salad at a wonderful takeout place near our office, called Agora. Chop everything well for ease of one-handed consumption.

2 cups (500 mL) kabocha squash or squash of choice, peeled, seeded and cut into ½-inch cubes

1 tablespoon (15 mL) + 2 teaspoons olive oil (10 mL), divided

1 teaspoon (5 mL) salt, divided

¼ cup (60 mL) pumpkin seeds

Pinch of chili flakes (optional)

1 bunch green or purple kale, ribs and stems removed and chopped (or 4 cups/1 L baby kale)

¼ cup (60 mL) Balsamic Vinaigrette (page 264), or to taste

2 tablespoons (30 mL) chopped fresh mint leaves

1 green onion, ends trimmed and thinly sliced

1 carrot, ends trimmed, peeled and ribboned

4 ounces (115 g) feta cheese, broken into chunks

½ cup (125 mL) black Kalamata olives, pitted and chopped

1 can (14 ounces/400 mL) chickpeas, drained and rinsed (optional)

Preheat the oven to 350°F (180°C). Line 2 baking sheets with a Silpat or parchment paper.

Place the squash in a medium bowl. Add 1 tablespoon (15 mL) of the olive oil and ½ teaspoon (2 mL) of the salt and toss to coat evenly. Arrange the squash in an even layer on one of the prepared baking sheets and roast until fork tender, about 20 minutes. Let cool to room temperature.

While the squash is roasting, place the pumpkin seeds in a small bowl. Add the remaining 2 teaspoons (10 mL) olive oil, remaining ½ teaspoon (2 mL) salt and chili flakes (if using) and toss to coat evenly. Arrange the pumpkin seeds in an even layer on the second prepared baking sheet and toast for 10 minutes, or until crunchy, stirring halfway through.

Place the kale in a large salad bowl. Massage the vinaigrette into the kale to soften the leaves. Toss in the roasted squash, toasted pumpkin seeds, mint, green onion, carrot, feta, olives and chickpeas, if using. Toss to combine.

Because kale is a sturdy green, dressed leftovers will still be good the next day, and probably on the day after that. Store leftovers in an airtight container in the fridge for up to 2 days.

GREEN PEPPER POT SOUP

Serves 2 to 3 as a starter

[E] This simple green soup is as soul-warming as the country it hails from. Our first trip with Ezzie was to Oracabessa, Jamaica, where she began developing a taste for Jamaican delicacies like stuffed cho-cho, festival and breadfruit. When she snuck a sip of my pepper pot soup, though, she looked pensive for a moment, then began swatting her tongue and shaking her head violently from side to side. So, maybe skip the Scotch bonnet pepper (or slice it fine and serve it raw as a garnish) if you're sharing with small ones. Pepper pot soup comes in many forms; this version is adapted from the recipe of a lovely Jamaican cook and friend named Errol Clemenston.

3 tablespoons (45 mL) unsalted butter or olive oil, divided

6 scallions, ends trimmed and roughly chopped

5 sprigs fresh thyme leaves

2 cloves garlic, minced

1 Scotch bonnet pepper (any colour), seeded and minced

2 small potatoes (any kind), peeled and quartered

3 cups (750 mL) vegetable or chicken stock

1 pound (450 g) spinach or callaloo, washed, trimmed, and roughly chopped

Salt

Crushed chili pepper, for garnish (optional)

In a large soup pot, warm 2 tablespoons (30 mL) of the butter over medium-low heat. Add the scallions, thyme, garlic and pepper, and cook, stirring occasionally, until everything starts to soften but not brown, about 5 minutes. Add the potatoes and stock. Cover and bring to a boil. Let boil, uncovered, for 10 minutes, or until the potatoes are easily pierced with a knife. Add the spinach and cook over medium heat until it is bright green and tender, about 5 minutes. Let cool for 10 to 15 minutes.

Working in batches, if necessary, transfer the soup to a high-speed blender or food processor and blend until smooth.

Return the soup to the pot and heat through. Season with salt, to taste, and stir in the remaining 1 tablespoon (15 mL) butter. Divide the soup among bowls. Garnish with crushed chili pepper, if desired.

GREENS AND CHEESE GRANDMA SLICE

Serves 4 to 6

[C] My love of pizza is an established and well-known fact. Round pizza, square pizza, pizza with red sauce, pizza with white sauce, vegetarian pizza, pepperoni pizza, any kind of pizza. Bread, sauce, cheese! It's my happy place.

   This is my riff on a traditional New York "grandma slice." It's also a perfect recipe, in those early days, to hand off to any newly minted grandma who happens to be nearby. If you have a batch of frozen dough or G-Ma feels like rolling up her sleeves, great; otherwise, most supermarkets sell pizza dough, and that works just as well. Feel free to swap out the toppings with whatever you have on hand—for me, arugula is always a must; the crunch and the peppery leaves keep the oozing cheese in balance and make me feel sort of like I'm having a salad.

1 batch Pizza Dough (page 252)

¼ cup (60 mL) Pesto Change-O (page 262)

1 cup (250 mL) Wilted Greens Forever (page 207), roughly chopped

4 ounces (115 g) stracciatella or buffalo mozzarella cheese, sliced

Handful of baby arugula

2 tablespoons (30 mL) extra-virgin olive oil

1 teaspoon (5 mL) red chili flakes

2 teaspoons (10 mL) flakey sea salt

Preheat the oven to 425°F (220°C). Grease a baking sheet with oil.

Using a rolling pin, roll out the pizza dough into a rectangular shape about the size of the baking sheet.

Carefully transfer the dough to the prepared baking sheet. Gently spread the pesto over the dough in an even layer. Arrange the wilted greens on top.

Bake for 12 to 14 minutes, until the crust is golden brown. Remove the pizza from the oven and place the cheese evenly on top. Return to the oven just long enough for the cheese to puddle a bit, 1 minute tops.

Top the pizza with the arugula, olive oil, chili flakes and salt. Serve warm if you can, but this pizza is also excellent served cold or at room temperature. Store leftovers in an airtight container in the fridge for up to 5 days. You can also cut the pizza into squares and freeze it in zip-top bags for up to 3 months.

HOW TO READ WITH ONE HAND

[E] When I feel my sanity slipping—a regular event, especially in the first year of mother-hood—the fastest remedy is to disappear into someone else's head for a minute. Even just a few pages of a book are enough to stop the spinning. "But I don't have time to read!" a part of you might protest. "Reading is a luxury I can no longer afford." To that part of you, which is also a part of me, I offer the following tactics.

In the earliest phase, when you have no hands for book-holding and frequent distractions make full-length audiobooks too ambitious, try short fiction podcasts. I used *The New Yorker*'s "Fiction" and "The Writer's Voice" podcasts as brain balm while nursing and doing the dishes.

If you decide to pump and are able to dock or hand off the baby while you do so, take advantage of that time. You have to tilt forward close to a power outlet anyway, so in the spirit of mise en place, you might as well turn your pumping station into a reading nook. All you need is a lamp (or one of those clever reading lights that clamp to the page) and a hands-free bra (weird-looking, life-saving), and you can inhale a few pages during the fifteen minutes it takes for the wheezy machine to do its job.

It's also helpful to scatter slim paperbacks and easily folded magazines anywhere you might be sitting when your baby falls asleep on you (and in the stroller, in case she nods off on a walk). If you spend hours picturing everything you have to do once the baby is sleeping—but then the instant the warm weight of her is curled up on your chest realize that you can't possibly go anywhere—you'll be glad to be able to pull a crumpled issue of *The Walrus* out from under a cushion. Bonus points if you've also stashed a tin of 2 AM Cookies (page 158) within reach.

This is an emotionally turbulent, sleep-deprived time, so you might not exactly be craving Dostoyevsky. Plan to read the literary equivalent of comfort food, and reread your favourites. That way, if you ever get one of those golden moments when you have two hands free and are overwhelmed by the possibilities—*I have twelve minutes; should I wash my hair, eat a grilled cheese, clean the house or try to "sleep while the baby is sleeping?"* (mad laughter)—you'll know what to do. You'll get right into bed with your book, and maybe a grilled cheese, and open up another world in your head.

- **By the pump:** *Calypso* by David Sedaris, *Paris to the Moon* by Adam Gopnik, *Tales of the Jazz Age* by F. Scott Fitzgerald, *The Gastronomical Me* by M.F.K. Fisher
- **Between couch cushions:** *The Girl Who Was Saturday Night* by Heather O'Neill, *French Exit* by Patrick deWitt, *The Dud Avocado* by Elaine Dundy, *The Pursuit of Love* by Nancy Mitford
- **Heavier (in terms of mass and subject matter), for when you're ready:** *The Golden Notebook* by Doris Lessing, the Neapolitan Novels by Elena Ferrante, *The Mandarins* by Simone de Beauvoir, *White Teeth* by Zadie Smith

TAMALE PIE WITH CORNBREAD CRUST

Serves 6

[C] This is one of the many recipes I grew up eating with no idea of its origins, until I Googled it to put in this book. It's basically a Tex-Mex shepherd's pie, and while I always kind of thought my mom invented it, she definitely did not—the recipe goes back to Texas in the 1900s. Although it's more of a casserole than a pie, the seasoned beef is lightly spiced and delicious and the cornbread makes it one of my favourite comfort meals.

TAMALE PIE FILLING

2 tablespoons (30 mL) olive oil

1 large yellow onion, diced

2 green bell peppers, diced

1 pound (450 g) ground beef

1 tablespoon (15 mL) chili powder

1 tablespoon (15 mL) ground cumin

1 tablespoon (15 mL) salt

2 teaspoons (10 mL) cocoa
   powder

1 teaspoon (5 mL) ground allspice

2 tablespoons (30 mL) tomato
   paste

1 cup (250 mL) water

1 cup (250 mL) canned tomatoes,
   chopped

2 ears corn, kernels removed and
   cobs discarded, or 2 cups
   (500 mL) frozen corn

1 cup (250 mL) sliced green olives

CORNBREAD CRUST

1 batch Hot Pepper Cornbread
   batter (page 219)

To make the tamale pie filling, in a large cast iron skillet or Dutch oven, heat the olive oil over high heat. Add the onion and peppers and cook, stirring occasionally to ensure that they do not burn, for about 5 minutes, until they start to soften. Add the beef, chili powder, cumin, salt, cocoa and allspice and continue cooking until the beef is browned and the vegetables are soft, about 10 minutes. Reduce the heat to medium. Add the tomato paste and cook for 2 to 3 minutes, until the colour changes from fire engine red to brick red.

Add the water, tomatoes, corn and olives. Bring to a boil. Reduce the heat to medium-low and let simmer, uncovered, for 20 minutes.

To make the cornbread crust, preheat the oven to 400°F (200°C).

Spread the Hot Pepper Cornbread batter evenly over the beef mixture in the skillet or Dutch oven.

Bake for 10 minutes. Reduce the heat to 350°F (180°C) and bake for an additional 20 to 25 minutes, until the cornbread is golden brown and a toothpick inserted in the centre of the cornbread comes out clean. Let cool for 10 minutes before serving.

Cover any leftovers with plastic wrap and store in the fridge for up to 5 days.

CHEATERS' CONGEE

Serves 4 to 6

[C] When I was in culinary school in New York, I lived a fifteen-minute walk past the last stop of the number 7 train in Flushing. To get home, I walked through the heart of Chinatown, and I never made it the whole way without stopping for some juicy dumplings, a crispy scallion pancake or a slurpy bowl of congee. I learned so much about food while living there, and developed a deep respect for rice. Congee, or "jook," is often served as a breakfast dish, but I like it any time of day, and it's become a staple for my daughters as well. This version was gifted to me by my friend Jaff Hom, who called it Cheaters' Congee. Instead of cooking it slow and low, he would boil the rice and then whisk hard to break it up and release its starch quickly. The result is a filling and warming porridge of sorts, which is also very fun to eat with the decidedly non-traditional (but delicious) addition of crushed up Fritos—a topping recommended to me by Jaff's dad, Mr Hom.

6 cups (1.5 L) water
1 cup (250 mL) long grain rice
1-inch (2 cm) piece fresh ginger,
    peeled and cut in half

FOR SERVING
1 cup (250 mL) shredded Roast
    Chicken in a Hurry (page 190)
3 to 4 scallions, ends trimmed and
    thinly sliced
2 tablespoons (30 mL) sesame oil
1 tablespoon (15 mL) soy sauce
Handful of Fritos or pork rinds,
    crushed

In a large saucepan, add the water, rice and ginger and bring to a boil over high heat. Reduce the heat to medium, cover and continue cooking, just above a simmer, for 45 minutes. Remove the lid and, using a large whisk, whisk hard for 1 to 2 minutes, until the rice has broken down a bit and the mixture starts to thicken. Reduce the heat to low and let simmer, uncovered, for an additional 10 minutes.

Divide the congee evenly among bowls. Top each serving with some chicken, scallions, a drizzle each of sesame oil and soy sauce and a sprinkle of crushed Fritos or pork rinds. Serve immediately.

Store leftovers in an airtight container in the fridge for up to 5 days. The congee will thicken as it cools, so when reheating you may need to add ½ cup (125 mL) water to thin it out.

TIP: For a more flavourful congee, cook the rice in 3 cups (750 mL) water and 3 cups (750 mL) vegetable or chicken stock. I don't like to use more stock than that because I don't want the flavour of the rice to be overpowered.

ALL THE SINGLE LADIES

[C] Part of being a single parent is that you can't tag out. There are two sides to that sword. Not relying on anyone else is liberating. You never have that moment when someone fails to meet your expectations, and you do that thing where you're trying to be relaxed about it but secretly are seething with resentment. You never get into a standoff over who unloads the dishwasher, whose turn it is to get up in the night or whose job it is to "project manage" the household. It's your turn. It's *always* your turn, and that's the other side of the sword.

"You're amazing!" people tell me, and though I'm grateful for the encouragement, I am definitely not amazing. I'm a regular person in an irregular situation. I am outnumbered. By my kids and by my dogs. I am also, usually, pretty tired. Still, I push forward, because the only way out is through. The way I get from point A to point B is not always smooth, or clean. My home decor will never be pinned. I am not aspirational. I am living my mistakes and my miracles, and it doesn't always feel good.

But your own strength will surprise you. There is no one else to carry the screaming toddler home from the park. You become handy, and let me tell you, running a bead of caulk around a bathtub is truly an enjoyable experience. Things break, and all it takes is a few YouTube videos and some confidence to set them right again. Smarter and more efficient than you used to be, you lug the clean laundry upstairs, and when you come back down you bring diapers to reset your mise en place. You are never empty handed. You look powerful and capable and exhausted.

It's going to be harder than you thought, but not as hard as doing it with someone who isn't the person you're meant to be with. Not as hard as doing it with someone who drains your batteries and leaves you empty and tired before the day has even begun. It's going to be hard, and you'll get through it. I promise.

WALK-IN TACOS

Serves 3 to 4

[C] Working in restaurants, there's often limited time to eat and definitely no time to sit down. In that way, it's comparable to being a new mother. These Walk-in Tacos take their name from a cooks' treat; you grab a wrap, go into the walk-in fridge and load up the wrap with whatever looks delicious and you can eat in about 30 seconds. (Bonus points if you eat this meal standing over a trash can with a roll of paper towel wedged under your armpit!) I've elevated this dish slightly, but at its heart it's the same low-output, high-impact meal being consumed behind the scenes in restaurants all over the globe.

TACO FILLING

2 tablespoons (30 mL) olive oil

1 medium yellow onion, thinly sliced

6 green bell or poblano peppers, seeded and thinly sliced

2 tablespoons (30 mL) water

½ cup (125 mL) plain cream cheese

1 tablespoon (15 mL) hot sauce

Pinch of salt

PICKLED CABBAGE

¼ head red or green cabbage, shredded

Juice of 2 limes

Pinch of salt

FOR SERVING

4 red radishes, ends trimmed and thinly sliced

1 jalapeño pepper, seeded and thinly sliced

2 handfuls of fresh cilantro, chopped

6 to 8 corn tortillas, warmed (see Tip)

2 avocados, pitted, peeled and sliced

½ cup (125 mL) Lime Crema (page 265)

To make the taco filling, in a medium skillet, heat the oil over medium-high heat. Add the onion and reduce the heat to medium. Cook for 5 to 7 minutes, stirring frequently, until the onion softens but does not brown. Add the peppers and cook for 15 to 20 minutes, stirring occasionally, until the peppers are tender.

Meanwhile, make the pickled cabbage. Place the shredded cabbage in a small bowl. Drizzle with the lime juice and salt and massage roughly so that the juice is absorbed and the cabbage becomes pickled. Set aside.

Return to the taco filling. Add the water to the skillet with the onion and peppers and cook on high heat for another 4 to 5 minutes, until the water has fully reduced. Add the cream cheese, hot sauce and salt, and stir until the cream cheese is melted. Turn off the heat.

To serve the tacos, in a small bowl, toss together the radishes, jalapeño and cilantro. Divide the tortillas among clean plates. Load each tortilla with about ½ cup (125 mL) of the pepper and onion mixture. Top each with a scoop of the radish, jalapeño, and cilantro mixture, some pickled cabbage, a couple slices of avocado and a drizzle of lime crema.

TIP: To warm the corn tortillas, you can throw them right on your ceramic stovetop over high heat. Once they start to char and bubble, flip them over and repeat. If you have a gas stove, set a skillet over high heat and use the same method. It's just as easy.

FATTOUSH WITH A SIDE OF FLATBREAD

Serves 4 to 6 portions

[C] This salad takes just a couple of minutes to assemble, and it can easily be eaten with a fork or loaded into a homemade flatbread or grocery store pita, should you wish to avoid forks altogether. Zhuzh it up with some smashed avocado, a schmear of Freezer Hummus (page 68) or a dollop of Tzatziki (page 261). The ground sumac adds a citrusy note, but it's okay if you don't have any—the salad will still taste great without it.

FATTOUSH

1 cup (250 mL) pita chips or stale pita bread, toasted

2 large seedless cucumbers, chopped

¼ cup (60 mL) pickled red onions (page 253)

4 vine tomatoes, chopped

½ cup (125 mL) crumbled feta

½ cup (125 mL) fresh mint, chopped

Zest and juice of 1 lemon

1 tablespoon (15 mL) ground sumac

¼ cup (60 mL) extra-virgin olive oil

Salt and pepper

FLATBREAD

½ batch Pizza Dough (page 252), room temperature

¼ cup (60 mL) extra-virgin olive oil, more for drizzling

2 tablespoons (30 mL) za'atar (optional)

To make the fattoush, in a large bowl, combine the pita chips, cucumbers, pickled onions, tomatoes, feta and mint. Season with the lemon zest and juice, sumac, olive oil and salt and pepper, to taste. Toss briefly, until evenly coated.

To make the flatbread, divide the pizza dough evenly into 4 to 6 balls, depending on how many people you will be serving. Oil each ball generously. Place the dough balls on a large dinner plate and let rise in a warm spot for about 15 minutes, until soft and puffy looking.

Set a barbecue or indoor grill to high heat. If you do not have a barbecue or indoor grill, preheat the oven to 475°F (240°C) and generously grease a baking sheet.

Place a metal bowl upside down on a clean countertop. Stretch a dough ball over the bottom of the bowl to make an oval shape. Season the dough on both sides with za'atar (if using).

If using a barbecue or indoor grill: Lay the dough over the hot grill. Cook for about 2 minutes, until the flatbread is charred but not burned. Using tongs, flip over the flatbread and cook the second side for another 2 minutes, or until the flatbread is charred but not burned. Transfer the flatbread to a clean plate and drizzle with olive oil. Repeat with the remaining dough balls.

If using an oven: Place the dough balls on the prepared baking sheet. Bake for 7 to 10 minutes, until golden and toasty.

Serve the fattoush and flatbread immediately.

FRIED HALLOUMI PLATE WITH GREEN BEANS, POTATOES AND JAMMY EGG

Serves 2, with leftovers

[E] At the peak of the one-hand phase, arranging versus cooking is often the name of the game, especially when it comes to the three lunches you might find yourself needing in an afternoon. Keeping hard-boiled eggs and cold, fried halloumi cheese (don't judge until you try it) in the fridge is recommended. Pre-cooking a few handfuls of finger-food vegetables like green beans and asparagus is also helpful. Salt them and keep them in the fridge wrapped in paper towel for easy grabbing.

8 to 10 small red or white potatoes, scrubbed

Salt and pepper

3 tablespoons (45 mL) Lemon Vinaigrette (page 263), more for serving

2 to 3 chives or a handful of fresh parsley leaves, finely chopped, more for serving

2 eggs

A big handful of green beans (about 20), ends trimmed

1 teaspoon (5 mL) extra-virgin olive oil

1 package (8 ounces/225 g) halloumi, cut into ½-inch (1 cm) slices

Handful of black olives

Prepare an ice bath (not for you, for the veggies and eggs) by filling a shallow dish with cold water and ice.

Place the potatoes in a small saucepan and cover them with water. Salt the water until it tastes like the sea. Bring to a boil. Reduce the heat to a simmer and cook for 15 to 20 minutes, until you can easily pierce the potatoes with a fork.

Reserving the water to cook the eggs, use a slotted spoon to transfer the potatoes to a small bowl. When the potatoes are cool enough to handle, cut them into halves or quarters, crack salt and pepper overtop and spoon on the vinaigrette. Garnish with the chives and toss to combine.

Bring the water back to a simmer. Using a slotted spoon, lower the eggs into the saucepan. Set a timer for 7 minutes. When the timer sounds, use the slotted spoon to transfer the eggs to the ice bath. This will stop the cooking and keep them jammy. Reserve the cooking water. To make the eggs easier to peel, rattle them around in the ice water, until they are a bit cracked up and are very cold. Remove them from the ice bath and sharply tap the bottom of each egg on a hard surface. Use your thumbnail to peel up from the bottom.

continues

Drop the green beans into the cooking water and simmer until they are bright green and cooked but still crunchy, about 5 minutes (you can always snatch one out of the saucepan and run it under cold water before taking a bite if you are unsure). Using a small strainer or tongs, lift them out of the water and drop them into the ice bath. Drain the beans. Season with salt, to taste, and set aside.

Place the olive oil in a small skillet over high heat. Fry the halloumi slices for 1 to 2 minutes on each side, until golden brown.

Divide the potatoes, eggs, beans and halloumi between 2 plates. Drizzle with additional vinaigrette, if desired. Sprinkle with chives and serve with black olives. Store leftovers (dressed or undressed), covered, in the fridge for up to 5 days.

TIP: Hard-boiled eggs can be incredibly frustrating to peel, but there's an air pocket at the bottom of the egg you can use to help you get a grip (literally and figuratively); always peel from the bottom up—it will make egg peeling (almost!) a breeze.

TURKEY TETRAZZINI

Serves 8 to 10

[C] I'm the first to admit I have major nostalgia for the mid-century casseroles I grew up eating. I rarely cooked them in my twenties, but once I was nursing, I craved the comfort and creaminess of a good ol'-fashioned baking dish full of beige food.

Salt and pepper

1 pound (450 g) spaghetti or fettuccine

2 tablespoons (30 mL) olive oil

2 cups (500 mL) button mushrooms, quartered

6 tablespoons (90 mL) unsalted butter

6 tablespoons (90 mL) all-purpose flour

2 cups (500 mL) chicken stock

1 cup (250 mL) heavy (35%) cream

1 cup (250 mL) whole (3.25%) milk

1 tablespoon (15 mL) Dijon mustard

½ cup (125 mL) grated asiago cheese

3 cups (750 mL) cooked turkey, cubed

½ cup (125 mL) roasted unsalted almonds, chopped

1 cup (250 mL) panko bread crumbs

Preheat the oven to 375°F (190°C).

Fill a large pot with water. Bring the water to a boil and salt it until it tastes like the sea. Cook the spaghetti according to package instructions. Drain, and spread the pasta out on a baking sheet to cool.

In a large cast iron skillet, heat the olive oil over high heat until shimmering. Add the mushrooms but do not stir. Reduce the heat to medium-high and let the mushrooms cook on one side until golden brown. Stir and continue cooking on medium-high heat until the mushrooms are golden brown all over. Remove from the heat and spread out on a baking sheet to cool. Season with salt and pepper, to taste.

In a large saucepan, melt the butter over medium-high heat. Sprinkle in the flour and reduce the heat to medium. Cook for about 5 minutes, using a rubber spatula to stir briskly all the while, so that the sauce won't taste like raw flour.

Switch to a whisk and continue stirring while you slowly add the stock, cream and milk. Cook for about 10 minutes, whisking continuously until the sauce is thick enough to coat the back of a spoon. Remove the saucepan from the heat. Stir in the mustard and cheese. Let cool for 5 minutes.

Add the turkey, spaghetti, almonds and mushrooms to the saucepan. Stir to combine. Transfer the mixture to a 9- × 13-inch (3.5 L) baking dish. Sprinkle the panko on top in an even layer.

continues

Bake for 30 minutes, until the sauce is bubbling and the panko is golden brown. Serve immediately. Store leftovers, covered, in the fridge for up to 5 days. Rewarm any leftovers in a covered baking dish at 375°F (190°C), or do what I do and eat them cold, straight out of the fridge. Like all good casseroles, this one holds together when chilled.

TIP: With recipes that call for Parmesan cheese, I often reach for asiago cheese instead. It's typically more affordable and slightly softer, so it's easier to grate and blends into sauces more quickly.

BROILED MAPLE CHAR

Serves 4

[E] Arctic char drizzled with maple syrup and cooked briefly over a hot fire is a very Canadian dinner. This is the indoor, weeknight-supper version, and it's ideal for feeding everyone fast. A cold-water fish mostly found in Iceland and Canada, char is a sustainable option and is more delicate than salmon, but if you can't find it, salmon will work just as well (though it will likely be thicker and take longer to cook).

12 ounces (340 g) Arctic char or salmon fillet
2 teaspoons (10 mL) pure maple syrup
Pinch of salt
Drizzle of extra-virgin olive oil
Lemon slices, for serving

Position a rack in the top third of the oven. Preheat the broiler to high. Line a rimmed baking sheet with foil. Important: Don't use parchment paper when cooking this close to the heat source. No fires, please.

Pat the fish dry. Place it on the prepared baking sheet, skin side down. Rub the fish with the maple syrup. Any syrup that drips down onto the foil will burn and create a bit of smoke, so try to avoid dripping. Season with a big pinch of salt and a drizzle of olive oil.

Broil for 6 to 10 minutes, or until the fish is opaque and just firm in the centre.

Serve with lemon slices alongside Wilted Greens Forever (page 207) and/or Lemon Caper Roasted Cauliflower (page 204). It's very good served cold the next day, too. Store leftover fish in an airtight container in the fridge for up to 2 days.

MOM GUILT

[C] I used to roll my eyes when people mentioned mom guilt. As if it were some sort of email chain you could opt out of. I naively assumed that it was external: pressure from society, family and frenemies to adhere to a certain script, societal norm or unachievable daily life. That's not mom guilt. *That* is mom shame—and although it can be easier said than done to tune out the unnecessary chirping of outside noise, it *is* possible.

But how do you tune yourself out? Mom guilt is something that bubbles up from within and comes without warning, sapping you of your confidence and making you question even the smallest decision.

[E] Mom guilt is what we torture ourselves with after leaving for work in the morning, once we've unclamped the tiny fingers from our arms and hair, cries of "MOMMY HUG!" still echoing in our hearts. It's what rips you apart while your most beloved person is screaming piteously in her crib in a desperate attempt to prolong the day, when all her little body needs is sleep.

There might not be an off switch on the part of you that tries to blame yourself for everything, regardless of whether those things are within your control. The acute moments, I've discovered, can be handled like the contractions of childbirth: by breathing through the pain and waiting for it to pass.

[C] Having children makes a lot of decisions clearer. There's a certain amount of JOMO (joy of missing out) that comes with this new territory, excusing you from exhausting social situations or family obligations you'd rather avoid. But the decisions that take you away from your children, from your people, aren't as easily made and often come with a linger-ing sense of regret. Or, in my case, with an ache in my chest that throbs until I swoop my girls up in my arms again. Choosing to go on that work trip, to escape to the gym for a couple of hours or even to book a weekend away (alone) because you are about to go batshit crazy after back-to-back bouts of some powerful head cold to which you also fell victim—it doesn't always feel like you are doing the right thing.

When I think about the big picture of my life now, and how I spend my time, I use the girls as my barometer. What will make me a better mother and playmate for them? What will reduce my stress? What will give me more energy? It doesn't wipe out the guilt, but it at least offsets it. Sometimes you just have to push through and do what needs doing, but that's not a forever state. Motherhood is.

KABOCHA SQUASH AND OLIVE OIL LOAF

Makes 1 loaf

[C] One of my favourite restaurants in the Santa Monica area introduced me to this amazing loaf. I tweaked some of the ingredient amounts and changed the method to make it easier for the home cook. However, if you're looking for a more authentic take on this recipe, open your smartphone, book a flight to LAX, go to Gjelina and buy a slice of the real deal.

1 small kabocha squash

2 cups (500 mL) all-purpose flour

1½ teaspoons (7 mL) baking powder

1 teaspoon (5 mL) baking soda

2 teaspoons (10 mL) ground cinnamon

1 teaspoon (5 mL) ground nutmeg

1 teaspoon (5 mL) salt

1¼ cups (300 mL) granulated sugar

3 eggs

¾ cup (175 mL) + 1 tablespoon (15 mL) extra-virgin olive oil, more for roasting the squash

1 tablespoon (15 mL) apple cider vinegar

1 cup (250 mL) dark chocolate chips

¼ cup (60 mL) raw pumpkin seeds

Preheat the oven to 425°F (220°C). Line a medium baking sheet with parchment paper.

Cut the squash in half, lengthwise. Use a large spoon to remove the seeds. Give the flesh a light drizzle with olive oil and place on the prepared baking sheet, cut side down. Roast for 20 to 30 minutes, until the squash collapses a bit and is easily pierced with a paring knife. Let cool, then peel off the skin and discard.

Preheat the oven to 350°F (180°C). Lightly grease a 10- × 6-inch (3 L) loaf pan and neatly line it with parchment paper.

In a large bowl, sift together the flour, baking powder, baking soda, cinnamon and nutmeg. Add the salt and stir to combine.

In a high-speed blender, combine the squash, sugar, eggs, olive oil and vinegar. Blend on high, until smooth. Using a rubber spatula, scrape the contents of the blender into the bowl with the dry ingredients. Fold together, until there are still some small pockets of flour visible, making sure not to overmix. Add the chocolate chips and pumpkin seeds. Stir until the flour is just incorporated.

Scrape the batter into the prepared loaf pan. Bake for 60 to 70 minutes, or until a toothpick inserted into the centre of the loaf comes out clean and the edges of the loaf start to pull away from the pan. Let cool in the pan for 10 minutes before transferring the loaf to a wire rack to cool completely.

Store the loaf in a zip-top bag in the fridge for up to 5 days or wrap tightly with plastic wrap and freeze for up to 3 months.

TIP: You can use about 1 to 1½ cups (250 to 375 mL) cubed and roasted sweet potato, butternut squash or acorn squash (really, any kind of squash except spaghetti squash) and no one will know the difference. You can also use an equal amount of canned pumpkin and skip the roasting altogether. Just be sure you don't accidentally buy pumpkin pie mix.

GINGER CAKE

Makes 1 (9-inch/1.5 L) round cake

[C] This isn't so much a cake as a giant shortbread biscuit studded with crystallized ginger, courtesy of my grandma Mildred. I prefer it slightly underbaked and, as in my biscuit recipe (page 39), freezing the butter and grating it ensures that it gets distributed evenly, without overmixing the dough and making it tough. This Ginger Cake is a great offering for someone else (especially around the holidays!) since it's extremely easy to bake and extremely delicious.

⅞ cup (220 mL) unsalted butter

2 eggs

2 cups (500 mL) all-purpose flour

1 cup (250 mL) granulated sugar

1 cup (250 mL) crystallized ginger slices

Pinch of salt

2 tablespoons (30 mL) ice water

Preheat the oven to 350°F (180°C). Lightly grease a 9-inch (1.5 L) smooth or fluted springform pan. Place the butter and a box grater in the freezer.

In a small bowl, beat the eggs. Transfer 2 tablespoons of the egg to a pinch bowl and set aside.

In a large bowl, sift together the flour and sugar. Once the butter is thoroughly chilled (about 15 minutes), place the box grater in the bowl of dry ingredients and quickly grate in the butter. Add the ginger, salt, the larger bowl of egg and the ice water. Using your hands, knead briefly to combine. The mixture will still be quite crumbly.

Transfer the batter to the prepared pan. Use your hand to pack it into the bottom of the pan, then prick with a fork all over. Brush the top with the reserved egg.

Bake for 30 minutes. Reduce the heat to 325°F (160°C) and continue baking for 15 minutes, until golden brown. Let cool to room temperature.

Store the cake in an airtight container in the fridge for up to 5 days or wrap tightly with plastic wrap and freeze for up to 3 months.

2 AM COOKIES

Makes 24 cookies

[E] I have never been so hungry in my life as I was during the first few months of motherhood. There was a stash of high-calorie nut and seed bars in my bedside drawer, and I would inhale one each night while nursing, clawing off the plastic wrap like a racoon. My dad, catching wind of this situation, quietly began making these oatmeal date cookies and bringing them over in a tin fitted with waxed paper. He visited every other day to hold his granddaughter, wearing his least scratchy wool sweaters and bearing a tin filled with half a dozen golden, chewy cookies. Now Ezzie and I make these together.

⅔ cup (150 mL) all-purpose flour

½ teaspoon (2 mL) baking soda

¼ teaspoon (1 mL) salt

¼ teaspoon (1 mL) ground cinnamon

¾ cup (175 mL) unsalted butter, room temperature

1 cup (250 mL) firmly packed brown sugar

½ cup (125 mL) granulated sugar

1 egg

2 tablespoons (30 mL) water

1½ teaspoons (7 mL) pure vanilla extract

3 cups (750 mL) rolled oats

1 cup (250 mL) pitted and chopped Medjool dates or dark chocolate chunks

Preheat the oven to 350°F (180°C). Line 2 baking sheets with parchment paper.

In a medium bowl, sift together the flour, baking soda, salt and cinnamon.

In a large bowl, use a wooden spoon to mix the butter, brown sugar and granulated sugar. Beat until light and fluffy. Add the egg and stir until well combined. Stir in the water and vanilla. Stir in the flour mixture, until well combined. Using your hands, mix in the oats and dates, until evenly distributed.

Using your hands or an ice cream scoop, roll the dough into golf ball–size balls. Arrange the dough balls on the prepared baking sheets 1 inch (2.5 cm) apart. Using the palm of your hand, gently press down on each dough ball.

Bake for 15 minutes, or until the edges are golden brown but the centres are still soft. Let cool to room temperature.

A FULL PLATE

The part when your baby (and then, suddenly, toddler) has joined the family table.

[E] Here you'll find our favourite recipes for the whole family, including several that we used early on to help our kids discover exciting tastes and textures. This chapter is about trying to create that magical scenario in which you're making dinner—something reasonably healthy and not too labour intensive—and the people you're planning to share it with, whether new or experienced eaters, are as jazzed as you are about what's cooking. If you're Christine, maybe one of your kids is even sitting on the counter biting into a raw onion to prepare her palate.

[C] My girls started eating food early. There were a few arched eyebrows (spoiler: there always are), but for me, the time felt right. I wasn't trying to hand them roasted turkey legs at four months, but I was giving them soft foods with strong flavours, such as Coconut Milk Rice Pudding (page 172), Red Lentil Dal with Spiced Onions (page 195) and Triple Mushroom Soup (page 186). They ate some of it and gummed on other things like oversteamed broccoli and carrots and, eventually, tinned fish. They are good eaters. They are actually great eaters, and for the most part, they take what I put in front of them in stride. It helps that we eat together. They see me take a shot of sauerkraut juice, and then they take a shot of sauerkraut juice.

I purposely started them on strong flavours early. I used to work at a restaurant in a vacation town on Nantucket Island, and I was saddened by the kids (and teenagers) who came in with their parents and ordered the $27 buttered farfalle. Not just because that's an exorbitant price for a $0.32 plate of food, but because those kids (and teenagers) were missing out on real food. Vegetables! Spices! Sauces! I want to be able to take my girls out to dinner and share one of life's greatest pleasures—good food—together.

My girls are not babies anymore, and their preferences have changed, but they still love the recipes in this chapter, and they love to cook with me, which has made my life at times more difficult but always more joyful. Waking up to Piper's face in mine yelling, "PANCAKES, MAMA!" is something that stops my heart, and despite whatever else I am forgetting to teach them, I feel proud that they can crack an egg or season a soup. From a purely practical standpoint, I like being able to cook one meal for all of us, which to me seems both efficient and convivial in equal measure.

THE GOOD

Makes about 2 cups (500 mL)

[E] This Greenhouse original developed by Jermaine Jonas is my all-time favourite green juice. Ezzie loves it, too; she's been known to grab the bottle from my hands, take a big swig and pronounce, "That one's good." It contains no sweet fruit, but unlike some of the meaner greens out there, it isn't the least bit swampy. Crisp cucumber and lemon brighten up the leafy greens, and the tiny pinch of salt, while not essential, underscores the natural saltiness of the celery for a bright, savoury finish.

8 cups (2 L) loosely packed
   spinach
8 large romaine leaves
½ cucumber, unpeeled, coarsely
   chopped
1 stalk celery, coarsely chopped
1 lemon, peeled and halved or
   quartered
Pinch of salt (optional)

Push the ingredients through your juicer a handful at a time. Strain the juice using a fine sieve, if desired. Add the salt (if using) and stir to combine. Serve chilled.

TIP: Don't have a juicer? Reduce the greens to whatever fits in your blender, add enough water to get things going and whiz everything together on high speed. Strain and serve over ice.

GREEN GINGER SMOOTHIE

Makes 1 large smoothie for mom and baby to share

[E] A smoothie is the perfect mom food. You can assemble, blend and drink it with one hand, and it makes vegetables taste like dessert, which is not a bad thing at any age. Plus, when 6 PM rolls around and you realize your one-year-old has eaten nothing but goldfish crackers and black olives all day, it's comforting to remember that she drank a great heap of greens first thing. The toppings listed below are delicious but optional depending on the chew skills of your child and what you have on hand.

1 frozen banana, roughly chopped (see Tip)

2 cups (500 mL) loosely packed baby spinach or kale

½-inch (1 cm) piece fresh ginger, peeled and chopped

1 tablespoon (15 mL) almond butter or Cinnamon Pecan Butter (page 257)

1 cup (250 mL) Vanilla Almond Milk (page 20) or milk of choice

TOPPINGS
Really Crunchy Granola (page 19)
Hemp hearts
Pumpkin seeds

Place the banana, baby spinach, ginger, almond butter and almond milk in a high-speed blender and blend on low until combined and then on high until smooth, about 30 to 45 seconds total.

Divide the smoothie between mom- and baby-size glasses. Top with granola and/or other crunchy bits, if desired.

TIP: If you don't have any bananas in the freezer, don't fret! Use a room-temperature banana instead and add ½ cup (125 mL) ice cubes to the blender along with the rest of the ingredients before you start blending. You can also decrease the sweetness of this smoothie by substituting ½ cup (125 mL) frozen raw cauliflower florets for ½ of the banana, if desired.

BREAKFAST COOKIES

Makes 8 to 10 large cookies

[C] Gluten-free, sugar-free, dairy-free. These are a snap to make, great to travel with and fairly forgiving if you want to load in extra superfoods like gojis or go in the other direction and dump in a fistful of dark chocolate chips.

1 cup (250 mL) Roasted Applesauce (page 256) or unsweetened store-bought applesauce

1 large banana

1 tablespoon (15 mL) apple cider vinegar

1½ cups (375 mL) rolled oats

¾ cup (175 mL) millet

2 teaspoons (10 mL) baking powder, sifted

½ teaspoon (2 mL) ground cinnamon

¼ cup (60 mL) roasted almonds, chopped

¼ cup (60 mL) pumpkin seeds

¼ cup (60 mL) dried fruit of choice, such as golden raisins or chopped figs

Preheat the oven to 375°F (190°C). Line a baking sheet with parchment paper.

Place the applesauce, banana and vinegar in a high-speed blender. Blend on high, until smooth.

In a large bowl, combine the oats, millet, baking powder, cinnamon, almonds, pumpkin seeds and dried fruit. Use a rubber spatula to scrape the contents of the blender into the dry ingredients. Stir until just combined.

Using your hands, separate the batter into 8 to 10 equal portions. Mould each portion into the shape of a burger patty. Arrange the cookies on the prepared baking sheet.

Bake for 10 to 12 minutes, until golden brown. Let cool on the baking sheet for about 5 minutes before eating. Store the cookies in an airtight container in the fridge for up to 5 days or freeze in zip-top bags for up to 3 months.

TIP: Add a handful of bran flakes, or whatever cereal bits are in the bottom of the bag, to the batter for some extra crunch. If the mix becomes a bit tight, just splash in some water, orange juice or milk to loosen it.

PANCAKES FOR THE PEOPLE

Makes 15 (3½-inch/9 cm) pancakes

[C] Pancakes feel special but, let's be honest, they aren't. Any recipe that was made by your great-grandparents, whether they were in a prairie sod house or hunkered down in a croft in the wilds of Newfoundland, was likely not a culinary feat. However, your children don't know that, and with a dusting of blueberries, sprinkles, chopped-up banana—or whatever is in the cupboard—you can transform any morning into something slightly magical for the little people hounding you for breakfast. This recipe is just as easy to make as a boxed mix, and it doesn't include any of the stuff you can't pronounce. It also has the added benefit of letting you control how much sugar and salt are added.

1 cup (250 mL) all-purpose flour

1 teaspoon (5 mL) baking powder

Pinch of salt (optional)

2 tablespoons (30 mL) unsalted butter, more for cooking

1¼ cups (300 mL) buttermilk

1 tablespoon (15 mL) granulated sugar, honey or maple syrup

1 egg, beaten

FOR SERVING (OPTIONAL)

Unsalted butter

Pure maple syrup

Honey

Lemon Curd (page 259)

Raspberry Chia Jam (page 257)

In a large bowl, sift together the flour, baking powder and salt, if using.

Melt the 2 tablespoons (30 mL) of butter. In a small bowl, whisk together the melted butter, buttermilk, sugar and egg. Add the buttermilk mixture to the bowl with the dry ingredients and, using a rubber spatula, stir in a figure-eight motion, until just combined, making sure not to overmix.

Heat a large skillet over medium heat. Add a pat of butter. Once the butter starts to shimmer, drop a few spoonfuls of batter onto the pan in different areas, making sure the spoonfuls don't run into each other. The batter should be fairly loose, and each spoonful will puddle into a round shape. Once air bubbles start to appear on the surface of the pancakes (after about 1 to 2 minutes), use a metal spatula to confidently flip each pancake over and allow them to brown evenly on the other side, about 1 to 2 minutes. Pancakes will be slightly puffed and springy to the touch when done. Transfer immediately to a clean plate. Repeat, adding more butter to the pan as necessary, until no batter remains.

Divide the pancakes among plates and add your favourite toppings, such as butter and maple syrup. Serve immediately. If you're batch cooking for later, let the pancakes cool completely on a wire rack before placing them in a zip-top bag. Freeze for up to 3 months.

TIP: Don't have time to Martha Stewart these pancakes or clean up after teaching your toddlers how to hold a whisk? Chuck the dry ingredients in a high-speed blender and pulse until combined. Add everything else and blend until just smooth (about 20 to 30 seconds). Cook as usual.

ON THE KINDNESS OF STRANGERS

[C] Until the girls were about six months old, I lived in a walk-up with a narrow and steep staircase. I couldn't open the stroller inside, so I had to put it out on the street. When I took the dogs for their daily walk I would bring down the stroller, open it outside, put the gear in and then go back upstairs, bring one baby down in her bouncy chair and set her inside the door at the bottom of the stairs with the door locked, and then get the other baby, unlock the door, put her in the stroller, buckle her in, and then load the other baby and buckle her in as well. Then I would open the door one last time to call down the dogs: Rocky, a three-year-old beagle-chihuahua–Jack Russell mix rescue dog from Korea, and Lucy, my massive six-year-old chocolate Lab.

On a very normal day that I otherwise would not remember through my haze of hormones and fatigue, I'd finally gotten everyone out the door. The dogs still weren't used to the stroller and would buck and pull in opposite directions. We'd made it about two blocks when Lucy stopped short in the middle of the road and proceeded to drop the biggest shit I have ever seen. The stroller lurched. Rocky pulled in the reverse direction. A car braked and the driver looked peeved while waiting for me to clear the intersection. I felt a wail bubbling in my throat and that telltale prickling of the eyeballs. Then, just as I was reaching for a dog poop bag, a man in full spandex on a bike came hurtling toward me.

Then a miracle happened. He stopped. He gracefully dismounted. He reached for the bag and said, "Let me get that for you."

This single act, this moment of a complete stranger stopping and stooping with a thin green bag wrapped around his hand, stands out as one of the kindest and most gracious things anyone has ever done for me.

The kindness of strangers is part of what makes those first few months bearable. Thank goodness that for every time someone says, "Oof! Double trouble, huh?!" or "Looks like you have your hands full!" there's also the sort of person who doesn't mind holding your baby so you can pee in a public restroom. Or the teenager who unexpectedly jumps up to help you lift your stroller off the bus, and to whom you mutter a thank you, even though he can't hear it through the pulsating EDM music coming out of his earphones. Or the woman you are convinced may just be an angel after she casually looks at you as you lug dogs and babies and suitcases out of a hotel in rural New Brunswick in a blizzard and says, "I shovelled off your car for you. Have a safe drive." And then there's every single person on a transcontinental flight who understands that the person having the worst time listening to your baby cry is you.

There are all sorts of things you learn about yourself when you become a parent: how you handle sleep deprivation; whether you are, in fact, organized; what your limits are (because you'll go way, way past them). But perhaps the most important thing I learned is how good people are. How much they want to offer you support. Not because they expect anything or because they feel sorry for you, but because we've all been there, helpless in the middle of the road, ready and hoping to accept help.

CASHEW CREAM OVERNIGHT OATS

Serves 4 to 6

[C] After the girls go down for the evening, I'm often torn as to whether I want to do something productive in preparation for the next day or just crash. Usually I split the difference and make one small thing (fortifying myself with a quiet glass of wine or a hot tea) that I know will pay big dividends in the morning. This is one of those recipes.

1 cup (250 mL) steel cut oats

2 tablespoons (30 mL) unsweetened shredded coconut

1 cup (250 mL) raw unsalted cashews

¼ cup (60 mL) pure liquid honey

1 teaspoon (5 mL) pure vanilla extract

¾ cup (175 mL) water

Pinch of salt (optional)

FOR SERVING

1 cup (250 mL) fresh berries, such as raspberries and blueberries

2 tablespoons (30 mL) pure liquid honey

Place the oats in a medium bowl and cover with hot water. Let soak for 1 hour. Rinse the oats under cold running water, drain and squeeze out as much excess moisture as possible. Transfer to a dry medium bowl and add the coconut.

Place the cashews in a high-speed blender. Add the honey and vanilla and pulse to combine. With the blender running on medium-high speed, slowly stream in the water. Increase the speed to high and blend until smooth.

Using a rubber spatula, scrape the cashew mixture into the bowl with the oats and coconut. Stir to combine. Taste and add a pinch of salt, if desired. Cover and refrigerate overnight to allow the oats to continue to soften.

To serve, divide the cold oats among bowls. Top with fresh berries and a drizzle of honey. Store leftover oats (ungarnished) in an airtight container in the fridge for up to 5 days.

COCONUT MILK RICE PUDDING

Makes 4 to 6 servings

[C] I started making this for my daughters as one of their very first foods. Most babies start on gruel-type food, but even the stuff in the organic aisle has ingredients that make me go *Hmmmm* . . . And let's be honest: it's also pretty expensive for what it is. I much preferred making my own and giving my daughters a chance to explore a bit of texture and optional toppings like Roasted Applesauce (page 256) or smashed-up berries. Unlike Pablum, this recipe is also adult friendly, and you can zhuzh it up with more elaborate (and crunchy!) add-ons like cacao nibs and dried mulberries while your baby gums on a softer version.

2 cups (500 mL) cooked long
    grain rice
2 cups (500 mL) full-fat coconut
    milk (see Tip)
1 cinnamon stick
2 tablespoons (30 mL) pure maple
    syrup or pure liquid honey
    (optional)
Pinch of salt

TOPPINGS (OPTIONAL)
2 tablespoons (30 mL) golden
    raisins
2 tablespoons (30 mL)
    unsweetened shredded coconut
½ mango, sliced

In a medium saucepan, combine the rice, coconut milk, cinnamon stick, maple syrup (if using) and salt. Bring the mixture to a boil, then reduce the heat to low and simmer for 15 to 20 minutes, until the rice has softened and the liquid has thickened. Let cool for 5 to 10 minutes (longer if it's for a baby).

You can serve the rice pudding warm or cold. Divide it among bowls and top with equal amounts of raisins, coconut and mango, if desired.

TIP: You can use any kind of milk for this (including breast milk, if you have a surplus!), but I do like the island vibes of coconut milk.

TIP: You can add lots of other goodies to these muffins: fresh cranberries, nuts, chopped banana, grated apple, citrus zest, pumpkin seeds, whatever. Just be sure you don't add more than about 1 cup (250 mL) total or the muffins will be too dense. Let your kids choose what they want to add and get them to help you do the final stir and they'll be more likely to get excited about eating them.

RAGAMUFFINS

Makes 12 muffins

[C] Really, what is a muffin but a cupcake without frosting? I love a good handheld snack, I love baking and I love fruit-studded breakfast items, but as someone who has worked in the restaurant industry for almost twenty years, I can tell you that the muffin you're buying as the "healthy" option is often loaded with sugar and oil. If you want to have a piece of cake, have a piece of cake and just enjoy it. If you want to have a muffin, try these. They aren't sweet and you'll notice a difference, but your children likely won't because they are children, and everything is new to them.

1 cup (250 mL) rolled oats

1 cup (250 mL) + 1 tablespoon (15 mL) all-purpose flour, divided

2 teaspoons (10 mL) baking powder

1 teaspoon (5 mL) baking soda

Pinch of salt (optional)

1 cup (250 mL) Roasted Applesauce (page 256) or store-bought unsweetened applesauce

⅔ cup (150 mL) unsalted butter or virgin coconut oil, melted

1 teaspoon (5 mL) pure vanilla extract

3 eggs, beaten

1 cup (250 mL) frozen blueberries

Preheat the oven to 375°F (190°C). Lightly grease a standard muffin tin with non-stick cooking spray. If using muffin liners, line the tin with the liners and spray again to ensure that the batter doesn't stick to the paper.

In a high-speed blender, pulse the oats until they are a fine powder. Add 1 cup (250 mL) of the flour, the baking powder, baking soda and salt (if using) and pulse to combine. Transfer the mixture to a medium bowl.

In the same blender, add the applesauce, butter, vanilla and eggs and pulse to combine. Scrape the contents of the blender into the centre of the dry ingredients. Stir until almost combined.

In a medium bowl, toss the frozen blueberries with the remaining 1 tablespoon (15 mL) flour. Gently fold the blueberries into the batter, making sure not to overmix or the batter will turn purple.

Divide the batter evenly into the prepared muffin tin. Bake for 17 to 20 minutes, until the centre of the muffins spring back to the touch. Let cool in the tin for 10 minutes before transferring the muffins to a wire rack to cool completely.

Store the muffins in an airtight container in the fridge for 5 days or freeze in zip-top bags for up to 3 months.

MOLASSES BROWN BREAD

Makes 2 (9- × 5-inch/2 L) loaves

[C] My mom somehow juggled three kids, a cat, one to two dogs and a husband, and still managed to get a hot meal on the table most nights. I keep trying to do the math to figure out how she wasn't a raging basket case, but she made it look relatively easy. A physiotherapist for twenty-three years, she went back to school when I was a teenager and got a PhD in biomechanics. You know, just casually, as one does. I'm a kid, a cat, a husband and a PhD short, but I did master her bread recipe, and you can too.

2¼ cups (550 mL) lukewarm water

¾ cup (175 mL) fancy molasses

2 tablespoons (30 mL) active dry yeast

1 cup (250 mL) rolled oats

1 cup (250 mL) mixed uncooked grains (millet, quinoa, bulgur, steel cut oats and/or bran)

1 cup (250 mL) whole wheat flour

½ cup (125 mL) sunflower seeds or pumpkin seeds

½ cup (125 mL) hazelnuts (optional)

1 tablespoon (15 mL) anise seed or fennel seed

½ cup (125 mL) olive oil, more for drizzling

1 tablespoon (15 mL) salt

3 cups (750 mL) + ¾ cup (175 mL) all-purpose flour, divided

In a large bowl, whisk together the water and molasses. Sprinkle in the yeast and let stand for 10 minutes.

Add the oats, grains, whole wheat flour, sunflower seeds, hazelnuts (if using) and anise seed. Using a large whisk, whisk for 2 to 3 minutes to combine. Loosely cover with a clean dish towel and let rest in a warm area for about 1 hour.

Remove the dish towel from the bowl. Whisk in the olive oil and salt. Sprinkle in 1 cup (250 mL) of the all-purpose flour and stir with a wooden spoon. Once combined, add 2 cups (500 mL) of the flour. Stir to combine. When the dough starts to resemble a ball, transfer it to a clean, floured surface like a countertop or a large cutting board. With floured hands, begin kneading the dough, adding up to ¾ cup (175 mL) flour if the dough becomes sticky. Continue kneading for 5 minutes, until the dough is tacky but no longer sticky and feels soft but not stiff.

Form the dough into a ball and drizzle with olive oil. Rub the oil all over the surface of the dough. Place the dough in a warm area, cover with a clean dish towel and let rise for 1 hour.

Punch down the dough and knead it on a clean, floured surface for 2 to 3 minutes. Drizzle the dough with oil and let rise, covered, for another hour.

continues

Preheat the oven to 350°F (180°C). Lightly grease 2 (9- × 5-inch/2 L) loaf pans with non-stick cooking spray.

Turn out the dough onto a clean work surface. Using a bench knife, divide the dough in half. Form the dough into 2 loaf shapes. Transfer the loaves to the prepared pans. Cover each with a clean dish towel and let rise for 20 minutes, until almost doubled in size.

Bake for 55 minutes, until the tops of the loaves are golden brown and they sound hollow when you tap them. Let cool in the pans for 10 minutes before transferring the loaves to a wire rack to cool completely. Store the bread in a zip-top bag at room temperature for up to 1 week or freeze for up to 3 months.

TIP: This recipe doesn't require a lot of active time, but it can be a bit annoying to have to babysit the dough in addition to whatever children you are in charge of. I'll often start this recipe mid-afternoon, and once I get my loaves in the pans, I put them in the fridge overnight for the final rise. Because they're cold, the rise slows down. Early the next morning I pull the loaves out of the fridge and let them sit on the counter for about half an hour before baking them as usual. Warm, fresh bread for breakfast always makes me feel like I've accomplished something (early!), and the girls go crazy for it because "we MADE it, Mumma!"

CHILAQUILES

Serves 4

[C] I'm a big proponent of introducing your children to strong-flavoured foods early. Curries, smelly cheese, bitter greens, spicy foods—get it in front of them, and even if they don't like it at first, they will eventually. Why? Because kids get hungry, and they get used to things, and hungry kids eat things they have gotten used to. It took a year of me putting wilted greens in my girls' food before they actually ate them, but guess what? Now they love wilted greens. So, don't worry if Mexican breakfast food doesn't seem like something your child is going to automatically reach for. Make the foods you want to eat and let them come around when they are ready.

Leftovers can be reheated easily in the same skillet and make a great filling for quick tacos and burritos. If you're not into a savoury breakfast, don't be shy about making this for dinner. It is just as delicious when eaten after noon.

3 tablespoons (45 mL) olive oil, divided
½ pound (225 g) mild Italian sausage, casings removed
1 small yellow onion, thinly sliced
1 medium green bell pepper, thinly sliced
1 small eggplant, diced
1 jar (16 ounces/450 mL) prepared green salsa
½ pound (225 g) good-quality corn chips
4 eggs
1 cup (250 mL) full-fat sour cream
1 medium Hass avocado, pitted, peeled and cubed
½ cup (125 mL) grape tomatoes, halved
1 ear corn, kernels removed and cob discarded, or 1 cup (250 mL) frozen corn
Small handful of chopped fresh cilantro

In a 12-inch (30 cm) skillet with a lid, heat 2 tablespoons (30 mL) of the olive oil over medium-high heat. Add the sausage and brown for about 5 minutes, until it is cooked on the outside but still pink in the middle. Use a slotted spoon to transfer the sausage to a clean plate. Set aside.

In the same skillet, combine the onion and pepper. Cook for 5 to 7 minutes, until the pepper softens and the onion is translucent. Add the eggplant and cook for an additional 5 minutes, stirring occasionally. Cover with the green salsa. Reduce the heat, cover and let simmer for 10 to 15 minutes, until the eggplant is tender. Return the sausage to the skillet along with the corn chips and cook for 1 to 2 minutes more, until the chips have softened.

In a small skillet, heat the remaining 1 tablespoon (15 mL) olive oil over high heat until it shimmers. Crack an egg into the oil and reduce the heat to medium. Fry the egg for 1 to 2 minutes, until the whites are set but the yolk is still runny. Gently place the egg on top of the chilaquiles. Repeat 3 more times.

continues

FOR SERVING

1 jalapeño pepper, seeded and
    sliced (optional)
Hot sauce (optional)
Good-quality corn chips

Add the sour cream to the chilaquiles in a few large dollops. Do your best to artfully arrange the avocado, tomatoes, corn and cilantro on top. Serve immediately, with jalapeño and hot sauce for the adults, if desired, and extra chips for dipping. Store leftovers in an airtight container in the fridge for up to 5 days.

TIP: This recipe is great for using up overripe produce like zucchinis, tomatoes and even squash. Just chop it up and throw it in with the onion and pepper. You can add an additional 1 to 2 cups (250 to 500 mL) of chopped veggies without it drastically affecting the flavour of the recipe or the cook time.

ON POSTPARTUM DATING

[C] A lot of the boxes I checked as a new mom made me feel empowered. I bought a house, took it apart, put it back together. I got laundry done, bills paid. I drank good wine on Fridays and shovelled my driveway when it snowed. Once—when the water to the top floor was shut off during renos—I lugged steaming pails of water up two flights of stairs and made myself a perfect hamburger and ate it in the bathtub, feeling like I was in a fancy hotel and not a construction zone.

But that doesn't mean I didn't feel intensely lonely. Postpartum is a time when you are deeply needed, more than any other time in your life, but that same need puts you on an island. Your focus is just a pinprick of light, where the only thing that matters is the tiny person(s) nuzzling your neck and making little grizzly noises while they grip your finger with surprising strength. One day, you look up and see the island for what it is.

I was thick-waisted and raw when I started online dating (again). I felt ugly but determined to get out there. Not because I wanted anything long term, per se, but because I needed someone other than my kids to touch me. I needed to wax my upper lip and make out in the front seat of a car and not feel like a dumpy mother of two, just for a night.

When Andrew picked me up, I'd already fortified myself with two fingers of scotch. We went to the local pub, where I proceeded to drink more Pinot Grigio than was wise. I basically carried all of my baggage into the pub with me, then unzipped it and showed him the guts of my life. I remember caring but not caring if he, specifically, liked me. I felt like I had to just get one date over with so my catharsis would be complete.

At the end of the night I poured myself into his (extremely clean) sedan, and he drove me home. As we pulled up in front of my house, I unclipped my seatbelt, thinking I'd already thrown the game with all of my truth telling and oversharing. I looked at him and said, "Are we going to do the thing?"

If I had spent less time talking that night, I might have realized sooner that I'd met someone, finally, who was (is!) amazing. The kind of guy who takes off his hat at the table, swings my kids around in a laundry hamper until they peal with laughter and always does the dishes when I cook. The kind of guy who, as a third date, came over and helped me deep clean my basement.

I didn't know any of that on the first night as we made out in his car. I felt like I was getting closure on a part of my life, and although that *was* happening, I was also starting something new and necessary.

There's this misconception that when you have a child, you are complete. You're a woman, after all, and you have, in a primal and even a biblical sense, fulfilled your role as procreator. And in many ways, you are different, a larger version of yourself, but you still need friendship and love. You still want to be touched the way you were before, and sometimes maybe more so, because it's reassuring that even though you've done this massive, body-distorting task, you are still the same person. You are still someone capable of making someone else's eyes sparkly.

It's not easy to put yourself out there. To see pictures from "before" and to shrug your shoulders and acknowledge that life is how it is, not how it was. But with risk comes reward, and the thing about hurtling yourself back into what can be considered less a dating pool and more a dating quagmire is that you are so much more likely to find someone who, right now, is someone you want to be with. Not someone who "has potential" or "needs a little work" but someone who meets you where you're at and fills you up, because there's just no time to put effort into someone who isn't already the person you want them to be.

ANTIPASTO PASTA SALAD

Serves 4 to 6

[C] This is another of my grandmother Mildred's classic recipes. I'm sure she clipped it out of a newspaper sometime in the '60s, but it's stood the test of time and makes regular appearances at picnics, potlucks and weekday dinners. I haven't yet met a child who doesn't like pasta, and this salad is like a little activity centre of strong flavours for them to explore.

PASTA SALAD

8 ounces (225 g) rotini

2 cups (500 mL) sliced fresh button mushrooms

1 can (5 ounces/140 g) tuna, drained

1 jar (10 ounces/280 g) marinated artichoke hearts, drained and quartered

4 ounces (115 g) pepper salami, diced

DRESSING

2 cloves garlic, minced

1 to 2 white anchovies, chopped

3 tablespoons (45 mL) red wine vinegar

½ cup (125 mL) extra-virgin olive oil

½ teaspoon (2 mL) dried oregano

Salt and pepper

FOR SERVING

1 to 2 tablespoons (15 to 30 mL) pepperoncini picante in olive oil (optional)

Small handful of fresh parsley, chopped

To make the pasta salad, bring a large pot of water to a boil and salt it until it tastes like the sea. Cook the pasta according to package instructions. Drain.

In a large bowl, combine the pasta, mushrooms, tuna, artichoke hearts and salami.

To make the dressing, in a small bowl, smash together the garlic and 1 anchovy, until they become a paste. If you like the salty and fishy punch anchovies bring, smash a second one into the mixture. Whisk in the red wine vinegar. Continue to whisk and slowly drizzle in the olive oil. Add the oregano and season with salt and pepper, to taste.

Pour the dressing over the pasta salad and toss until evenly coated. Cover and let marinate for at least 30 minutes in the fridge or overnight.

Add the pepperoncini (if using) and toss the salad. Garnish with the parsley before serving. This salad tastes great the next day and can be stored in an airtight container in the fridge for up to 5 days.

TIPS: I don't think my grandmother even knew what bocconcini was, but I'm confident she would have approved of me adding some of those heavenly little cheese balls to this salad or, alternatively, some cubes of mozzarella. I don't think she'd mind if you felt inclined to add some either. About ½ cup (125 mL) would be the perfect amount.

Whenever I use fresh herbs, I like to add them at the very end so that they stay bright and crisp and don't get lost in whatever I'm cooking.

TRIPLE MUSHROOM SOUP

Serves 4 to 6

[C] What is it with kids and mushrooms? If I had to guess, I'd say it's the texture, since most people overcook mushrooms to the point of sogginess and, on a primal level, I think most of us don't like slimy foods. A properly cooked mushroom is a beautiful thing and a great way to introduce children to the depth of flavour and nuances that our little fungi buddies have. Soup takes a bit of the guesswork out of cooking mushrooms, and when this one is paired with some crusty bread and a drizzle of olive oil, it's like a friendly mushroom hug and a great way to introduce a new food to even the most discerning young palate.

3 tablespoons (45 mL) olive oil

1 medium yellow onion, peeled and quartered

1½ pounds (675 g) button mushrooms

4 ounces (115 g) shiitake mushrooms, caps only

5 fresh sage leaves

2 cloves garlic, smashed

½ cup (125 mL) dried porcini mushrooms

2 cups (500 mL) chicken stock or water

2 cups (500 mL) almond or cashew milk

Salt and pepper

FOR SERVING
Extra-virgin olive oil
Crème fraîche (optional)
Freshly cracked black pepper

In a large saucepan, heat the olive oil over medium heat. Add the onion and cook for 5 to 7 minutes, until translucent. Increase the heat to medium-high and add the button and shiitake mushrooms. Cook for about 5 minutes, stirring occasionally, until the mushrooms brown a bit and release some of their liquid. Add the sage and garlic and cook for an additional 2 minutes. Add the porcini mushrooms, stock and almond milk. Increase the heat to high and bring to a boil, then reduce the heat to medium-low. Cook, uncovered, for 20 minutes, stirring occasionally.

Working in batches, if necessary, transfer the soup to a high-speed blender or food processor and blend until smooth. Season with salt and pepper, to taste.

Divide the soup among bowls and serve hot with a drizzle of extra-virgin olive oil or a dollop of crème fraîche, if using. Garnish with freshly cracked black pepper.

Store the soup in an airtight container in the fridge for up to 5 days or freeze in zip-top bags for up to 3 months.

BEEF GOULASH WITH BUTTERED EGG NOODLES

Serves 4 to 6

[C] Growing up, this traditional Hungarian stew was always served the day after a Sunday roast. While having her morning coffee, my mom would cut up what was left of the meat, slice some onions and dump the rest of the ingredients (including a generous squirt of ketchup) into our slow cooker. We'd all return from work or school to a mouth-watering smell and I'd tear off my bulky snowsuit and "check" to see if it was done (read: wolf down several large chunks of tender, hot meat). There are many versions of goulash; my recipe has a few nods to my mother's but omits the ketchup and brings in some deeper Old World flavours.

1½ pounds (675 g) stewing beef, cut into 1-inch (2.5 cm) chunks
Salt and pepper
2 tablespoons (30 mL) olive oil
1 carrot, cut into 1-inch (2.5 cm) chunks
1 small celeriac, cut into 1-inch (2.5 cm) chunks
2 medium yellow onions, thinly sliced
4 cloves garlic, thinly sliced
4 cups (1 L) beef stock (homemade or low sodium)
1 can (28 ounces/800 g) diced tomatoes
3 bay leaves
2 tablespoons (30 mL) Hungarian sweet paprika
1 tablespoon (15 mL) packed brown sugar (optional)
5 sprigs fresh thyme, tied together with kitchen twine
8 ounces (225 g) dried egg noodles
2 tablespoons (30 mL) unsalted butter

FOR SERVING
¼ cup (60 mL) full-fat sour cream
½ cup (125 mL) chopped fresh flat-leaf parsley

Using paper towel, pat the meat dry and then season aggressively with about 2 teaspoons (10 mL) of salt and 1 teaspoon (5 mL) of pepper. In a large Dutch oven, heat the olive oil over high heat. Reduce the heat to medium-high and, working in batches, add the beef to the hot oil and brown evenly on all sides. Set the beef aside on a large plate.

In the same Dutch oven, add the carrot and celeriac and cook for 5 minutes, stirring occasionally, until the vegetables start to caramelize. Add the onions and garlic and cook for an additional 2 to 3 minutes. Add the stock, beef, tomatoes, bay leaves, paprika, brown sugar (if using) and thyme. Increase the heat to high and bring to a boil. Reduce the heat to a simmer and cook, uncovered, for 90 minutes to let the sauce reduce. Cover the goulash and cook for an additional 30 minutes, until the beef and vegetables are tender. Remove the thyme bundle and bay leaves from the pot and discard.

Bring a large pot of water to a rolling boil over high heat and salt it until it tastes like the sea. Cook the egg noodles according to package instructions. Drain and toss with the butter.

Divide the egg noodles among bowls. Serve the goulash over the noodles. Add a dollop of sour cream to each bowl and garnish with parsley. Store leftover goulash and noodles separately in airtight containers in the fridge for up to 5 days.

ROAST CHICKEN IN A HURRY

Makes 1 roast chicken

[C] Don't try this one if you have a weird spill on the bottom of your oven. Or, if you're like me and are incredibly stubborn and want to cook the best chicken ever despite that weird spill, do yourself a favour and open your doors and put on the oven fan, hood fan—or really, any fan—first. I was skeptical about this method, but then I tried it and I will never cook a chicken any other way. The skin comes out unbelievably crisp, the centre is still juicy and full of flavour and it's just so quick—you can go from zero to roast chicken in about 30 minutes. And hey, it might inspire you to clean your oven more often.

1 small chicken (about 2 to 3 pounds/0.9 to 1.35 kg), room temperature

Salt and pepper

½ small yellow onion

A few sprigs of fresh thyme, rosemary or sage (optional)

2 cloves garlic, smashed

3 to 4 potatoes, cut into wedges (optional)

Preheat the oven to 500°F (260°C)—yes, that is the correct number. Spray a medium roasting pan with cooking spray (this will make clean-up easier). Weigh your chicken and make a note of how many pounds it is.

Liberally sprinkle the whole chicken with salt and pepper, inside and out. After seasoning the cavity, stuff it with the onion, fresh thyme (if using) and garlic. If there is an excess of skin or fat around the cavity, trim it off and discard.

Arrange the potatoes (if using) on the bottom of the roasting pan. Nestle the chicken onto the potatoes. Roast for 10 minutes per pound, plus 5 to 10 minutes, or to an internal temperature of 165°F (74°C). If you don't have a thermometer, that's okay. I don't have one either. Just give the thigh a little poke with a paring knife and check to make sure the juices run clear. Let the chicken rest out of the oven for about 10 to 15 minutes before serving.

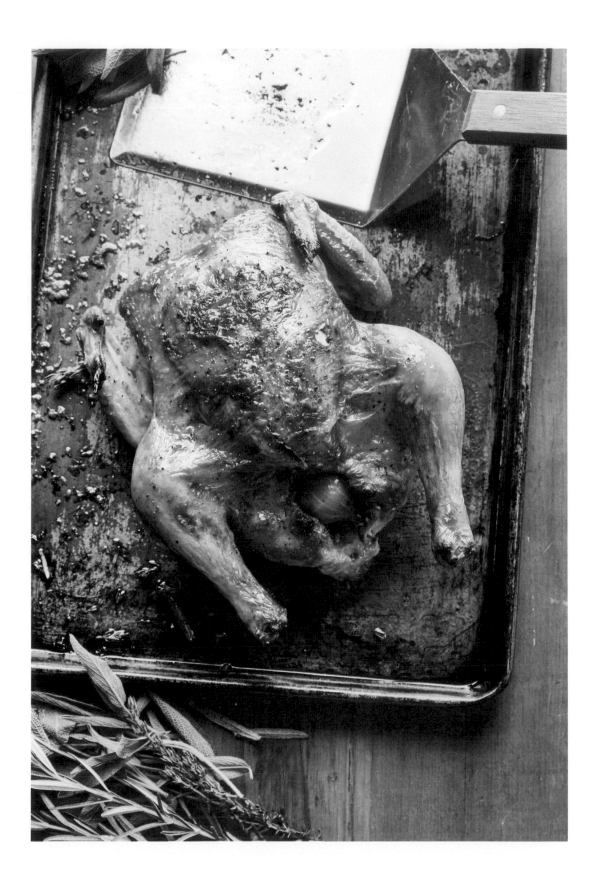

MULLIGATAWNY

Serves 8 to 10

[C] My grandmother Marge's recipe for Mulligatawny, a dish that has many variations from its roots in Southern India, calls for the cooked rice to be added *to* the stew. You can absolutely make it this way, but unless you eat the entire batch in one sitting, you'll notice that the rice sucks up all the liquid if it sits overnight and you'll be left with more of a porridge than a stew. I prefer to keep it separate and to let my girls "build a bowl" with rice, some stew and whatever toppings and garnishes they feel like using that day. The spice level of this recipe is very mild (trust me, Marge was from Strasbourg, Saskatchewan, and not an adventurous eater), but feel free to toggle the heat level up or down as you like by putting in more or less chili.

2 tablespoons (30 mL) unsalted butter

3 stalks celery, diced

2 carrots, diced

2 large Spanish onions, diced

1 large sweet potato, peeled and diced

4 cloves garlic, minced

1-inch (2.5 cm) piece fresh ginger, peeled and minced

1 small red bird's eye chili, thinly sliced

4 teaspoons (20 mL) curry powder

1 teaspoon (5 mL) ground turmeric

½ teaspoon (2 mL) ground nutmeg

8 cups (2 L) chicken or vegetable stock (homemade or low sodium)

3 cups (750 mL) diced cooked chicken or turkey

2 Granny Smith apples, peeled and grated

Zest and juice of 1 lemon

1 cup (250 mL) plain Greek or Skyr yogurt, more for serving

Salt and pepper

In a large saucepan, melt the butter over medium-high heat. Add the celery, carrots, onions and sweet potato. Reduce the heat to medium and let the vegetables sweat, uncovered, for about 10 minutes, stirring occasionally, making sure they do not brown.

Add the garlic, ginger and chili. Cook for 2 to 3 minutes. Add the curry powder, turmeric and nutmeg and cook for 2 to 3 minutes, stirring continuously, to ensure that the spices toast but do not brown.

Add the stock and increase the heat to high. Bring to a boil, then reduce the heat to low and let simmer for 15 to 20 minutes, until the vegetables are tender. Add the chicken, apples, lemon zest and juice and yogurt and stir to combine. Season with salt and pepper, to taste.

Serve hot over rice. Top each bowl with a dollop of yogurt and fresh herbs. Store leftover stew in an airtight container in the fridge for up to 5 days.

TIP: With any chunky soup or stew like this one, I love to throw in a handful of hearty greens at the end for colour and flavour. For heartier greens, like broccolini or collards, keep cooking for a minute or two, but for spinach or baby kale simply turn off the heat, add the greens and cover for a minute or so before stirring the wilted greens into the soup.

FOR SERVING

4 cups (1 L) cooked long grain rice

½ cup (125 mL) chopped fresh
   flat-leaf parsley or cilantro

TIP: If you are in an extreme hurry to make dinner, you can put the dried lentils in a blender and pulse them until they are the texture of cornmeal. They will cook much faster, in about 15 minutes instead of 1 hour, but the consistency of the dal will be more or less the same.

RED LENTIL DAL WITH SPICED ONIONS

Serves 4 to 6

[C] Although I love lentils, the best part of this recipe is arguably the spiced onions, so don't hold back and don't be shy about loading up your kids with my favourite allium. If you're looking to make this a whole meal and not just a side, throw in 2 cups (500 mL) sliced Savoy cabbage with the sliced onions to fry, and serve it with hot Flatbread (page 252), a dollop of yogurt and some rice so that your kids can make "tacos."

DAL

2 tablespoons (30 mL) ghee or
   olive oil
3 yellow onions, diced
2 tablespoons (30 mL) tomato
   paste
1 cup (250 mL) red lentils
3 bay leaves
1 cinnamon stick (optional)
5 cups (1.25 L) chicken stock
   or water
Salt

SPICED ONIONS

2 tablespoons (60 mL) ghee or
   olive oil
2 onions, thinly sliced
Large pinch of salt
Pinch of ground cinnamon
Pinch of ground nutmeg
Pinch of ground cumin
Coriander seeds (optional)

FOR SERVING

2 cups (500 mL) cooked long
   grain rice
Lime wedges
½ cup (125 mL) chopped fresh
   cilantro

To make the dal, in a large Dutch oven, heat the ghee over medium-high heat. Add the onions and reduce the heat to medium. Cook for about 5 minutes, stirring gently, until the onion is translucent. Add the tomato paste and cook for 2 to 3 minutes, until the colour changes from fire engine red to brick red. Add the lentils, bay leaves and cinnamon stick, if using. Stir to combine. Add the stock, increase the heat to high and bring to a boil. Let bubble aggressively on high for about 10 minutes. Reduce the heat to medium-low and simmer, stirring occasionally, for 1 hour. Give the lentils a final stir. Fish out the bay leaves and cinnamon stick and discard. Season with salt, to taste. Transfer the dal to a large serving dish.

To make the spiced onions, give the Dutch oven a quick rinse and a wipe and return it to the stove. Place the ghee in the Dutch oven and set over high heat. Once the oil starts to shimmer, add the onions. Spread them out in an even layer so that they brown but do not burn. Reduce the heat to medium-high. Season the onions with the salt, cinnamon, nutmeg, cumin and coriander seeds, if using. Let the onions fry, without stirring, until they are golden brown. Do your best to flip the onions over, so that those that were on the top are now on the bottom. Continue frying until the onions are a fairly even golden brown, about 5 to 7 minutes.

Spoon the spiced onions and their delicious oil over the dal. Serve over rice with lime wedges and top with chopped cilantro.

SAAG PANEER (WITH TOFU OPTION!)

Serves 4 to 6

[C] Spinach is one of those foods that kids don't always take to right away. I remember my parents making some really, truly dreadful creamed spinach when I was a kid, and it took me a long time to recover from that. I'm still not one of those people who can eat a bowlful of raw spinach with a handful of Craisins and balsamic vinaigrette. But puréed into a sauce and served with some hot cheese? I can get behind that. Though not traditional, we offer vegan substitutions for the cream and paneer with cashew milk and tofu, respectively.

2 tablespoons (30 mL) ghee or
  olive oil
2 to 3 cloves garlic, smashed
1-inch (2.5 cm) piece fresh ginger,
  peeled and thinly sliced
6 to 8 cups (1.5 to 2 L) loosely
  packed spinach, divided
Pinch of ground nutmeg
Pinch of ground cinnamon
Pinch of ground cumin
Pinch of red chili flakes
1 teaspoon (5 mL) salt
1 cup (250 mL) heavy (35%)
  cream or cashew milk
1 pound (450 g) paneer or firm
  tofu, cubed
2 teaspoons (10 mL) black pepper
2 teaspoons (10 mL) fresh lemon
  juice

In a large skillet with a lid, heat the ghee over medium-high heat. Add the garlic and ginger and cook for about 5 to 7 minutes, until golden brown. Add about half of the spinach and cook until wilted, about 2 to 3 minutes. Add the nutmeg, cinnamon, cumin, chili flakes and salt. Pour in the cream and stir. Cook for 1 additional minute.

Working in batches, if necessary, transfer the spinach mixture to a high-speed blender or food processor and blend until smooth. Return it to the skillet and increase the heat to high. Add the paneer and cook until warmed through. Once the paneer is hot and the sauce has just barely started to thicken, add the remaining spinach and turn off the heat. Cover for 1 to 2 minutes to allow the spinach to wilt. Finish with the black pepper and lemon juice.

Serve hot alongside Red Lentil Dal with Spiced Onions (page 195) or Red Pepper Curry Chicken (page 94). Store leftovers in an airtight container in the fridge for up to 5 days.

RED RICE AND BEANS

Serves 4 to 5

[C] This is one of those delicious recipes that many cultures have a version of. When you work in a kitchen, it's often one of the dishes present at family meal because it's inexpensive, quick to prepare and filling. For many of the people I have worked alongside over the years, whether they were from Jamaica, El Salvador or Cuba, it also represents a taste of home—and I do believe that's the best taste there is.

2 tablespoons (30 mL) extra-virgin olive oil

1 small yellow onion, diced

2 cloves garlic, minced

1 to 2 anchovies, chopped (optional)

1 tablespoon (15 mL) capers, chopped

1 teaspoon (5 mL) sweet Spanish paprika

Pinch of salt

2 tablespoons (30 mL) tomato paste

1½ cups (375 mL) long grain rice

2 cups (500 mL) water

1 can (15 ounces/425 mL) black beans, drained and rinsed

In a medium saucepan, heat the olive oil over medium-high heat. Add the onion and reduce the heat to medium. Cook, stirring gently so that they soften but do not brown, for 4 to 5 minutes. Add the garlic, anchovies (if using), capers, paprika and salt. Stir to combine. Cook for 2 to 3 minutes.

Add the tomato paste and cook for 2 to 3 minutes, until the colour changes from fire engine red to brick red. Add the rice and stir to coat it evenly with the tomato paste mixture. Add the water and bring to a boil. Cover, reduce the heat to low and simmer for 17 minutes. Remove from the heat. Dump the beans on top of the rice, return the lid to the saucepan and let the heat from the rice steam the beans. After about 5 minutes, fluff the rice and stir to incorporate the beans.

Serve hot alongside Roast Chicken in a Hurry (page 190) or Walk-in Tacos (page 141). Store leftovers in an airtight container in the fridge for up to 5 days.

INVASIVE SPECIES

[E] At home, I don't like chaos. Attempting to control my domestic surroundings has been a tendency since childhood. Outdoors, Mother Nature rules supreme. But inside my four walls, I ache for things to be clean, dry and at right angles.

The kitchen is where I am at my most neurotic. If I'm alone, before sitting down to dinner I will wash all the dishes I used to cook, except the plate I'm eating from and the fork I'm using.

Having a baby when you're this mess-sensitive is a questionable plan. Late in pregnancy, I showed a photo of my future daughter's bedroom to my uncle Alan. Anthony and I had stayed up most of the previous night assembling her furniture, a task I'm now convinced is part of a covert parental training program (lessons five through seven: fine motor skills, nocturnal patience and restraint that will keep you from killing one another down the line), and I was excited to share the news that her rug was machine washable.

"This is how it looks now, before there's spit-up everywhere," I explained.

My uncle looked at the photo on my phone and then up at me. "You know, you could just get a doll," he said.

But it was too late for that. In a few short weeks, we would welcome a small, professional sower of chaos.

After Ezzie was born, predictably and by necessity, I relaxed my standards. I was too tired to care about right angles. Maybe I relaxed too much. Or maybe Mother Nature decided to smite me and my tidy-house hubris. In any case, armies arrived.

The mice were first. They gnawed through the bags of pasta, panko, fenugreek and flour in our pantry. We found humane traps; they found a way to eat the cheese and run. We didn't see them, but every night we left cheese, and every morning it was replaced with their thank-you pellets.

I docked Ezzie in one of our now-propagating colourful baby devices and sanitized the drawers, the cabinets and the cupboard under the sink. Over the course of an hour or two, our kitchen became thoroughly inhospitable. But still, they visited.

Then I spotted one—and it was upstairs. At first, it struck me as being cute, with its little mouse ears. As a kid, I'd watched a show about mice that live in a library; maybe this one had come upstairs to find a good novel. But that thought was soon replaced by another, less charitable one: upstairs is where Ezzie wiggles on her play mat, pulling the string that makes the owl go *Hoo, hoo* and convincing us she's a child genius. Upstairs is where she sleeps. Upstairs is unacceptable, you little punk.

I spoke to Anthony, who has better sang-froid than I do. He called in the pest patrol.

As Ezzie grew, her capacity for sowing chaos increased, and the parade of uninvited guests continued. Now she could pull books from the shelf and rip out plot points. On Sunday mornings, I had to read the paper quickly before she shredded it. But still there was a language barrier between us. Still she screamed for hours at a stretch, usually in the evenings, without being able to tell us why. We called it colic and then teething, but with hindsight I now know it was a remedial unit in the parental training program designed for those most resistant to having their lives upended (lesson seventy-three: this child owns you now; stop fighting it).

That spring, a family of raccoons created an illegal rental unit under our back deck. We turned a blind eye at first, even as their renovations required deinsulating parts of our basement, but once all parties were old enough to travel, we installed a kind but firm one-way door.

By summer, the carpenter bees (a misnomer: these ones were in the demolition business) had set up shop in our pergola, burrowing destabilizing holes into the heavy wooden structure above Ezzie's head while she splashed in her paddling pool.

With each new wave, I felt my hypocrisy more keenly. I wanted to love all of Earth's creatures (they all have mothers!), but I also wanted to keep them the eff away from my tiny daughter.

By the time the cockroaches rolled in, Ezzie was eating solid food with gusto—and throwing it at the walls and rugs with even greater gusto. Though I still spent a lot of time chasing her with a dustbuster, we now spoke the same language ("Challah down!" she'd shout as she tossed her toast), and I was beginning to feel philosophical about our guests.

In French, *avoir le cafard,* or "having the cockroach," is a satisfying way to express gloom. You can use it to complain about an annoying task—"Picking dried smoothie off the wall, *le cafard*"—or to describe your overall mood if things aren't going so well.

Although we still had a few bugs, I realized *le cafard* had departed. I had relinquished the illusion of control. Mother Nature had taught me that my precious walls were well within her jurisdiction. Hadn't I even served as her conduit recently, when I could have just got a doll?

If the parade of unwelcome pets was just another unit in the parental training program, perhaps I was finally within reach of a passing grade. So, we've got an insect or two? Soon we'll have long-haired kids throwing soccer balls at lamps, I reasoned into thin air. If they're hungry, let them make themselves a snack.

GRILLED VEGETABLE HEAVEN WITH WHIPPED RICOTTA

Serves 2 as a light meal, 4 as a side

[E] Grilled eggplant and zucchini can be either melt-in-your-mouth miraculous or tough and gamey. Soaking sliced eggplant and zucchini in heavily salted water (the simplest form of brine) before grilling is one way to encourage tenderness. This works with chicken breast, too. Cook the vegetables at a high temperature and make sure every slice gets cooked through. This dish is delicious served with a thick piece of sourdough toast.

2 Japanese eggplants, cut in half lengthwise

2 zucchinis, sliced on the diagonal into ¼-inch (5 mm) rounds

1 cup (250 mL) ricotta cheese

3 tablespoons (45 mL) olive oil, divided

1 sprig rosemary, leaves separated and chopped

Salt and pepper

FOR SERVING
Toasted pumpkin seeds (page 126)
Extra-virgin olive oil
2 slices sourdough or bread of choice, toasted

Fill a large bowl with room-temperature water and salt it until it tastes like the sea. Place the eggplant and zucchini in the bowl and let soak for 30 minutes at room temperature. Drain, then pat the vegetables dry using a clean tea towel. If time is of the essence, you can skip soaking the vegetables, but they might not come out quite as tender.

In a food processor, purée the ricotta with 1 tablespoon (15 mL) of the olive oil, the rosemary and a pinch of salt for 1 to 2 minutes, until light and fluffy.

In a cast iron grill pan, heat the remaining 2 tablespoons (30 mL) olive oil over high heat. When it starts to shimmer, place the eggplant in the oil, flesh side down, and arrange the zucchini in a single layer (you may need to grill in batches). Cook for 5 to 6 minutes, until the bottoms get nice and brown. Using tongs, flip each piece of eggplant and zucchini and cook through, about 5 to 6 minutes more. Use a lid to keep spattering to a minimum. If grilling in batches, transfer the cooked vegetables to a rimmed baking dish and keep warm in the oven.

Using a spatula, divide the ricotta between 2 plates. Arrange the roasted veggies overtop. Season with salt and pepper, to taste. Garnish with the pumpkin seeds and more olive oil (always more olive oil) and serve immediately with sourdough toast on the side.

LEMON CAPER ROASTED CAULIFLOWER

Serves 4 to 6

[C] I tend not to jump on trends, partially because I live in a bubble of raising two children and two dogs, and partially because I can't be bothered to care. So there are no recipes for cauliflower pizza crust or cauliflower chocolate chip cookies, but this is a very good (and easy!) recipe that celebrates roasted cauliflower with its nutty texture and caramelized moreishness and then smothers it in a loosely French-by-way-of-Italy lemon caper vinaigrette.

¼ cup (60 mL) golden raisins, chopped

2 small heads cauliflower, quartered

¼ cup (60 mL) + ½ cup (125 mL) extra-virgin olive oil, divided

1 teaspoon (5 mL) salt

½ cup (125 mL) fresh lemon juice

2 tablespoons (30 mL) Dijon mustard

1 tablespoon (15 mL) pure maple syrup

¼ cup (60 mL) capers, chopped

FOR SERVING

¼ cup (60 mL) fresh flat-leaf parsley, chopped

Preheat the oven to 475°F (240°C).

In a small bowl, cover the raisins with hot water and let stand while you prepare the other ingredients.

In a large bowl, toss the cauliflower with ¼ cup (60 mL) of the olive oil and the salt. Arrange the cauliflower, cut side down, on a baking sheet. Roast the cauliflower for 15 to 20 minutes, until decisively charred.

In the same large bowl, whisk together the lemon juice, mustard and maple syrup. Slowly pour in the remaining ½ cup (125 mL) olive oil, whisking all the while. Drain the raisins and add to the dressing along with the capers. Whisk to combine.

Pour the dressing over the cauliflower. If serving immediately, garnish with chopped parsley. You can also let the dressed cauliflower marinate in an airtight container in the fridge overnight and serve either cold or at room temperature the next day. Simply platter the cauliflower and remember to garnish with the parsley before serving. Store the dressed and ungarnished cauliflower in an airtight container in the fridge for up to 5 days.

TIP: If you want to go a little more *bonjour* and a little less *ciao* with this recipe, swap out the ½ cup (125 mL) olive oil in the vinaigrette for an equal amount of warm brown butter. Because butter is solid when it's chilled, be sure to serve this version of the recipe warm or, if serving the next day, toss it in a hot skillet to warm slightly and make everything taste *incroyable*.

WILTED GREENS FOREVER

Serves 4 as a side

[C] I can't help myself: I put greens in almost everything. If it's a soup, stew, sauté or scramble, odds are I'll serve it to you with a fistful of greens added at the end. Sometimes I even wilt greens into my greens. It's a sort of compulsion, but one that keeps our taste buds exploring and brings in sharp flavours and bitterness (the good kind!) to balance out our meals.

It may seem like this recipe calls for a lot of olive oil, but here it is not only used for cooking, but also as a dressing when paired with the lemon juice.

2 very large bunches broccoli rabe, washed, dried and woody ends removed

¼ cup (60 mL) extra-virgin olive oil, more for serving

2 to 3 cloves garlic, smashed

2 tablespoons (30 mL) chicken stock or water

1 teaspoon (5 mL) red chili flakes

Juice of 1 lemon

Salt and pepper

¼ cup (60 mL) freshly grated Pecorino Romano cheese, for garnish (optional)

Separate the stalks of the broccoli rabe from the leaves. The stalks take a bit longer to cook; by separating them, you can cook them first so that they are tender just as the leaves wilt.

In a large cast iron pot or Dutch oven with a lid, heat the olive oil over medium-high heat. Once the oil begins to shimmer, drop in the garlic and cook for 3 to 4 minutes, stirring occasionally so that it becomes golden but does not burn.

Increase the heat to high and drop in the broccoli rabe stalks only. Stir-fry for 4 to 5 minutes, so that they cook evenly. When poked with a paring knife, they should offer up a bit of resistance, but not much. Add the leaves and give them a quick stir. Add the stock, cover and cook for 1 minute. The greens should be wilted and the leaves tender. Remove from the heat. Add the chili flakes and lemon juice and season with salt and pepper, to taste. Toss to coat evenly.

Serve the greens alongside Roast Chicken in a Hurry (page 190) or a generous slab of Eggplant Parmesan (page 50). Garnish with Pecorino, if desired. I like to use a rasp grater to grate the cheese over the greens at the table for my girls. We call it "cheese snow," and anything that gets them excited about a giant bowl of bitter greens, I'm here for.

Store the greens in an airtight container in the fridge for up to 5 days. Because of the lemon juice, they will discolour slightly but still be delicious, and they're great chopped up and added to Greens and Cheese Grandma Slice (page 130), Chicken Noodle Soup, Sort Of (page 76) or even High Acid, Deep Green Salad (page 125).

SPANISH TORTILLA

Serves 4 to 6

[C] Spanish cuisine does not have the same cachet as that of the baguette-toting cousins to the northeast, but it's definitely one of my favourite regions for food. Spanish food is simply prepared, with very fresh ingredients and lots of olive oil. This recipe is pure goodness and comes together quickly, especially if you have "helpers" to crack your eggs.

½ cup (125 mL) extra-virgin
  olive oil
2 medium yellow onions, sliced
  ¼-inch (5 mm) thick
2 medium yellow potatoes, sliced
  ¼-inch (5 mm) thick
2 teaspoons (10 mL) kosher salt,
  divided
8 eggs, beaten just enough to
  break up the yolks

Preheat the oven to 325°F (160°C). Lightly grease a 9-inch (1.5 L) round baking dish with non-stick cooking spray and trim a piece of parchment paper to sit neatly in the bottom of the dish.

In a large skillet with a lid, heat the olive oil over medium heat. Add the onions and potatoes and stir gently to coat them in oil. Season with 1 teaspoon (5 mL) of the salt. Reduce the heat to medium-low and cover. Cook for 20 to 30 minutes, stirring occasionally so that the potatoes do not stick, until the potatoes are tender but not falling apart.

Transfer the onions and potatoes to a large bowl. Add the eggs and the remaining 1 teaspoon (5 mL) salt. Stir, until evenly coated. Transfer the mixture to the prepared dish and bake for 25 to 30 minutes, until the edges are firm and the centre just barely jiggles.

You can serve the tortilla warm alongside some Wilted Greens Forever (page 207), but I think it is even better the next day, served cold, with a tin of fish and a High Acid, Deep Green Salad (page 125). Store the tortilla in an airtight container in the fridge for up to 5 days.

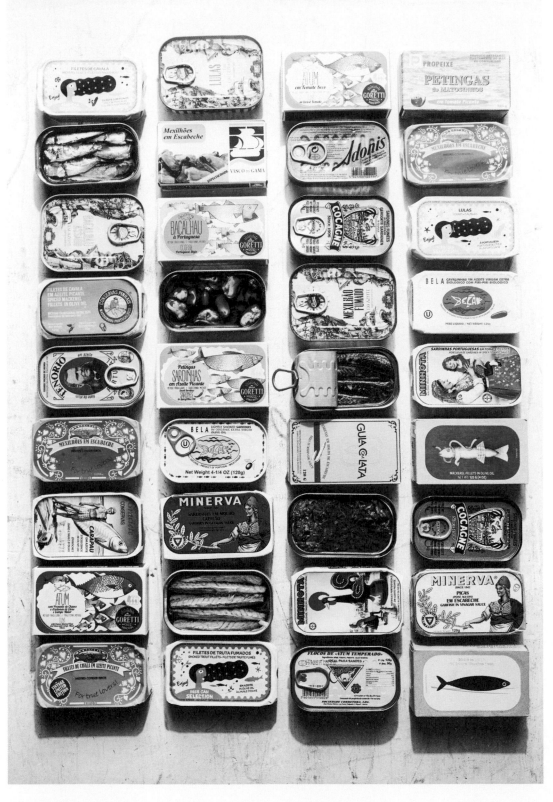

COMFORT ME WITH TINNED FISH

[C] It may seem out of place in a cookbook to recommend a small package of food that is already prepared and perfect, but tinned fish is more than just the sum of its parts. Tinned fish has been a supporting character in my life as a parent. I'm not talking about those dry cans of flaked light tuna, which require equal parts mayonnaise and fish to even be edible. I'm talking about plump mussels swimming in spicy vinegar, shimmering pale cod in olive oil and perfect, tiny sardines tucked into piri piri sauce, all resting in their iconic metal beds.

When I was pregnant and bracing myself for the possibility of an indeterminate period of immobility, I snatched up a seat sale to Spain. Feeling a bit like a sardine myself on the flight, I wedged my sizeable four months pregnant–with–twins belly into my seat, slid the seatbelt to the largest setting and sat packed tightly between two very tall men, careful to keep my elbows from spilling into their space when the in-flight meal came around.

I spent the next eight days or so tottering around Barcelona and San Sebastián, munching on croquettes, sipping sidra and seeking out provisions for the months to come. I shoehorned myself into shops that were so small they felt more like dollhouses but that somehow managed to contain endless teetering shelves of brightly wrapped packets of fish. By the time I returned, my half-empty suitcase was jammed with as many tins as customs would allow (and maybe one or two hunks of funky cheese). The usual suspects were there, of course, but also a few novelty finds: octopus stuffed with rice, skate with pickles in oil, cod and chickpeas enrobed in tomato sauce—all of which would provide sustenance, variety and comfort in the months ahead as I became more and more reluctant to leave the house. Once my shoes stopped fitting at about thirty-four weeks, my passion for cooking (or standing, for that matter) started to dwindle. My appetite, however, only accelerated, and I could often be found more or less horizontal on my sagging couch with a tin of fish perched on my growing stomach and a heel of bread at the ready for dunking.

After the girls were born, being able to crack a tin (clumsily, but still with one hand) and have an instant picnic with a handful of greens and a few counter tomatoes was not just useful but cheerful. People could drop in and I'd always have a half a bag of rye crackers, some olives and a few tins to spread around. Nothing fussy, just good hospitality. A bottle of something or other would be opened, and I'd keep a stack of napkins handy; I never failed to drip at least some fish oil onto the head of an unsuspecting newborn as conversation flowed around and through us.

Having been baptized with fish oil early, those not-so-newborns were soon gumming down tiny fish as well. I had bought a small home outside the city and slowly began disassembling it at night while Piper and Matilda slept. For months there were no floors on the main level, let alone a kitchen. Plus, I was still on maternity leave, and after buying diapers and formula, there wasn't much left for groceries. My daughters had watched me open enough cans of Riga Sprats to be curious, so I willingly shared. Finding a food that is affordable, convenient and delicious in equal measure is truly a blessing for any expectant or new mother. Bonus points when that food is also considered a "superfood."

Not that long ago, I took the girls to the library. I remember passing a shelf of young adult books and thinking, *One day, they will have read all of these.* I felt hopeful and excited and a little sad because my babies are growing up and away from me more every day. Then, a few days later, we were ordered to stay home and self-isolate because COVID-19 had wrapped up the world in a pandemic.

How do you teach your children about the world when it's only as large as the room you are in? Currently, Piper and Matilda can't even travel to the supermarket, let alone Spain. I think back to the heavy shelf of books I was convinced they would read, yes, but also forward, only ever in minutes or hours, to the next meal we will share. I do not think beyond that.

And so, tinned fish is supporting me again. It helps me make buttered toast more exciting, it works its way into spaghetti with lemon and bread crumbs and, yes, occasionally I even mix it with equal parts mayonnaise for a quick tuna melt. Spooned with its delicious oil onto a bed of greens, tinned fish helps me make our world bigger.

To give myself or the girls something, maybe from my travels but maybe just from my home on the east coast, is a small but tangible joy. I love watching them pick a tin of fish to share, as they hold each one up like a jewel to the light and pore over all the images. Then comes the initial explosion of forks and hands and mess everywhere. With fish oil all over their faces and hair slicked back like a couple of grinning seal pups, they remind me what good food does to a person: it makes you want to dive in and swirl crusty bread into the corners of your bowl to get every last morsel. To travel, to stay in, to challenge your circumstances or to just move forward. The best things, tinned fish reminds me, come in small packages.

COTTAGE PASTA

Serves 6 to 8

[C] This is the thing you make when you arrive at a travel destination and everyone is hungry and making noise, and you find yourself in the unenviable position of having to cook the exact moment you step through the door. Fear not! You may feel like Old Mother Hubbard, but if you can locate a forgotten box of pasta and a can of tomatoes in the cupboard—and perhaps pull most of an onion and a hard piece of cheese from your purse—you can make a delicious meal quickly. Par-cooking the pasta and then finishing it in the sauce helps save time but also makes for better flavour. In terms of options and ways to elevate this recipe, it's a bit of a choose your own adventure, and you really can't go wrong. Here, I suggest ricotta and spinach, but other classic combos include buffalo mozzarella cheese and arugula or Boursin cheese and wilted kale. Just don't put the cheese in too early or it will dissolve into a rosé sauce (unless that's your thing). Go a step further and throw in a handful of shrivelled black olives, some briny capers or even a chopped up sausage or two.

1 pound (450 g) penne, rigatoni or
    fusilli
4 tablespoons (60 mL) olive oil
1 medium onion, thinly sliced
2 cloves garlic
2 cans (28 ounces/800 g each)
    diced tomatoes, plus 1 can of
    water
4 cups (1 L) spinach
1 cup (250 mL) ricotta cheese
Small handful of fresh basil
Salt and pepper

Fill a large stockpot with water. Bring the water to a boil and salt it until it tastes like the sea. Cook the pasta according to package instructions, less 2 minutes. You want the pasta to be undercooked so that when you finish it in the hot tomato sauce, it will be perfectly tender. Drain the pasta but do not rinse it. Spread it out on a large baking sheet and let cool.

In the same large stockpot you used to cook the pasta, heat the olive oil over medium heat. Add the onion and cook for about 3 to 4 minutes, stirring occasionally to ensure that it does not brown. Briskly smash the garlic with the flat of a knife and add it to the pot. Cook the onion and garlic for an additional 4 to 5 minutes, until translucent. Add the tomatoes, then fill a tomato can with water and add the water to the pot. Increase the heat to high and bring to a boil. Reduce the heat to medium-low and simmer until the liquid has reduced by half, about 10 to 15 minutes.

Add the pasta to the pot and cook until almost tender, 1 to 2 minutes. Toss in the spinach to wilt. Turn off the heat. Stir in the cheese and basil. Season with salt and pepper, to taste. Serve immediately.

Store leftovers in an airtight container in the fridge for up to 5 days.

CHEESY POLENTA

Serves 4 to 6

[C] I often serve polenta in lieu of pasta with similar toppings. Pile it up with roasted veggies, plop on a meatball or two and some red sauce or smother it in charred mushrooms and Wilted Greens Forever (page 207). You can't go wrong. It's also delicious on its own, as pictured here, with just a drizzle of olive oil and a few rasps of cheese, which makes it a great option for a quick adult meal or as a first or early food, since minimal chewing is required.

4 cups (1 L) water
½ cup (125 mL) extra-virgin
   olive oil
1 cup (250 mL) medium grind
   cornmeal (I like Bob's Red Mill)
1 cup (250 mL) finely grated
   Pecorino Romano cheese
Salt and black pepper

In a large heavy-bottomed saucepan, bring the water and olive oil to a boil. Using a large whisk, slowly whisk the cornmeal into the water and olive oil mixture. Continue whisking until the polenta becomes thick and you need to switch to a rubber spatula. Once the polenta starts spitting at you, cover and reduce the heat to low. Cook for 20 to 30 minutes, stirring occasionally so that it does not stick to the bottom of the saucepan. When it's done, the polenta should be thick and almost fluffy. Turn off the heat and stir in the Pecorino. Season with salt and pepper, to taste.

Serve immediately alongside Wilted Greens Forever (page 207) or Summer Vegetable Succotash (page 30). Store leftover polenta in an airtight container in the fridge for up to 5 days.

TIPS: I like my polenta quite loose, but you can reduce the amount of water to 3½ cups (875 mL) for this recipe.

Instead of serving right away, pour it into a lightly greased baking dish, cover and allow it to set in the fridge overnight. The polenta will become firm enough to slice, and you can cut it into whatever shape you want (rectangles, cubes, stars, dinosaurs!). The polenta can be served cold, or you can pan-fry or grill it for some texture.

Kids seem to like dipping (I think it's an autonomy issue), so I usually serve it with a runny egg or some kind of creamy dip such as Lime Crema (page 265) or Tzatziki (page 261) and let the girls go wild.

HOT PEPPER CORNBREAD

Makes 1 (8-inch/2 L) square pan

[C] Anyone who has worked with me over the last two decades knows I love cornbread. It's so deceptively simple, and I love dunking it in soups, grilling it to serve alongside summer tomatoes and, of course, using the leftovers for stuffing.

2 tablespoons (30 mL) unsalted butter

2 shallots, minced

1 to 2 jalapeño peppers, minced

1 cup (250 mL) all-purpose flour

1 cup (250 mL) medium grind cornmeal (I like Bob's Red Mill)

¼ cup (60 mL) granulated sugar

1 teaspoon (5 mL) baking powder

1 teaspoon (5 mL) baking soda

1 teaspoon (5 mL) salt

½ cup (125 mL) canola oil

2 eggs

½ cup (125 mL) whole (3.25%) milk

½ cup (125 mL) full-fat plain yogurt

Preheat the oven to 425°F (220°C). Lightly grease an 8-inch (2 L) square pan with cooking spray.

In a small skillet, melt the butter over medium heat. Add the shallots and jalapeños and continue to cook until soft, about 4 to 5 minutes. Set aside.

In a large bowl, sift together the flour, cornmeal, sugar, baking powder, baking soda and salt. In a medium bowl, whisk together the oil, eggs, milk and yogurt. Add the shallots and jalapeños and whisk to combine. Pour the wet ingredients into the dry ingredients. Using a rubber spatula, fold in the dry ingredients, scraping down the sides and bottom of the bowl to ensure that no pockets of flour remain.

Transfer the batter to the prepared pan and bake for 20 to 25 minutes, until the cornbread is golden brown and the edges start to pull away from the pan. Let cool for 5 to 10 minutes before eating.

Store the cornbread in an airtight container in the fridge for up to 5 days or wrap tightly with plastic wrap and freeze for up to 3 months. To reheat, I recommend putting it in a warm skillet with about 1 tablespoon (15 mL) butter to take the chill off.

TIPS: You can swap out the canola oil for an equal amount of melted butter, olive oil, melted virgin coconut oil or any neutral oil without much discernable difference in flavour. Use what you have on hand!

If you like your cornbread cheesy, fold a handful of shredded Monterey Jack, mozzarella or sharp cheddar cheese into the batter before transferring it to the pan to bake.

POLENTA PEACH CAKE

Makes 2 (9-inch/1.5 L) round cakes

[C] There's something both necessary and wonderful about a recipe you can knock together with a few pantry items and whatever is slowly going soft in your fruit bowl. I recommend peaches for this recipe, but you would do just as well to rescue some sad-looking apples, pears or plums. Because this cake has a high fruit-to-cake ratio, it makes two (!) cakes, so you can give one to your neighbour and really make it look like you have your life together, or you can wrap it tightly in plastic wrap and freeze it.

½ cup (125 mL) medium grind cornmeal

1½ cups (375 mL) all-purpose flour

1 teaspoon (5 mL) baking soda

1 teaspoon (5 mL) salt

1 cup (250 mL) granulated sugar

½ cup (125 mL) unsalted butter, room temperature

3 eggs

½ cup (125 mL) full-fat plain yogurt

¼ cup (60 mL) extra-virgin olive oil

1 tablespoon (15 mL) chopped fresh rosemary leaves, or 3 to 4 drops rosemary essential oil (optional; see Tip)

7 medium ripe peaches

Mildred's Yogurt Sauce (page 258), for serving (optional)

Preheat the oven to 350°F (180°C). Grease 2 (9-inch/1.5 L) round cake pans.

Place the cornmeal in a large bowl. Sift in the flour, baking soda and salt.

In a medium bowl, cream together the sugar and butter until pale and fluffy. Beat in the eggs, one at a time.

In a small bowl, whisk together the yogurt, olive oil and rosemary, if using.

Add about half of the flour mixture to the bowl with the butter and sugar mixture. Stir until just combined. To the same bowl, add about half of the yogurt mixture. Stir until just combined. Repeat, making sure not to overmix or the cake will become tough.

Divide the batter evenly between the prepared cake pans. Cut the peaches in half and remove the pits. Firmly press the fruit, skin side down, into the batter.

Bake for 40 minutes, or until the edges of the cake start to pull away from the pan. Let cool in the pan for 20 minutes before transferring to a wire rack to cool completely. Serve on its own or with a dollop of Mildred's Yogurt Sauce (page 258), if desired.

Store the cake in an airtight container in the fridge for up to 5 days or wrap tightly with plastic wrap and freeze for up to 3 months.

TIP: Using essential oils is a quick way to add flavour to a recipe. Source high-quality, food grade organic oils such as rosemary, orange, lemon and cinnamon and use them in place of conventional spices or zest.

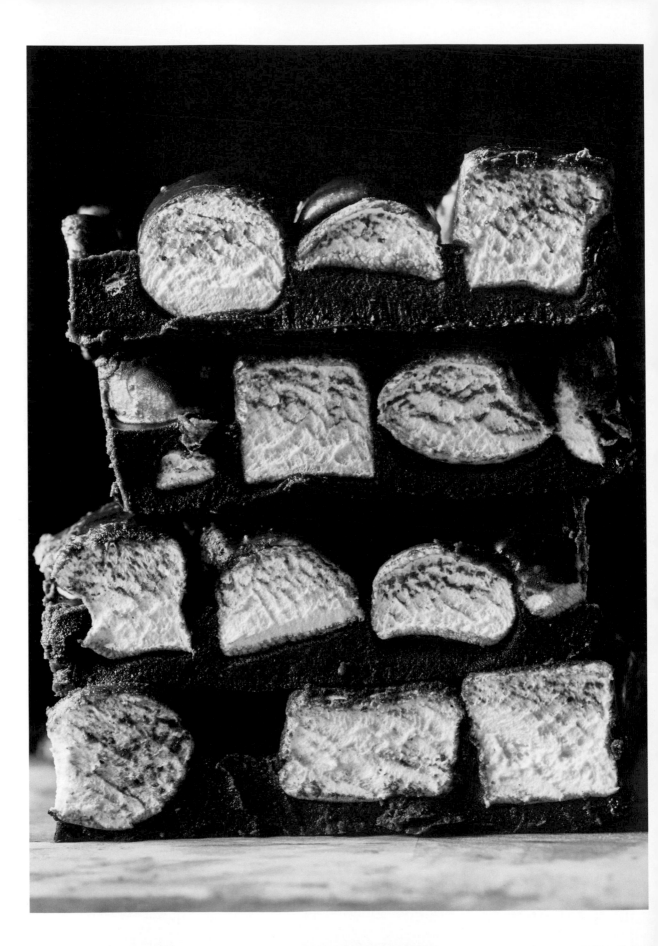

PEANUT BUTTER MARSHMALLOW SQUARES

Makes 16 squares

[C] I grew up loving road trips because my mom would make all kinds of delicious, sort of junky and definitely janky foods. At the time, I didn't realize it was a frugality measure. With three kids (and sometimes a cat or dog or both), it made sense that we loaded up the minivan anytime we had to travel and that my mom spent a couple of days prepping so we could save on airfare and overpriced fast food.

Being a single mom with twins, I've continued this tradition, also more or less out of necessity since one person cannot travel with two infants on any major airline. Now that the girls are older, it's just prohibitively expensive to fly, and more gear is required than I can heft on my own. Besides, who doesn't love firing up a great playlist, eating travel snacks and being out on the open road with toddlers?! These squares are my favourite. They are also the most decadent and most "I'm on a road trip!" treat in my repertoire.

2 cups (500 mL) dark chocolate chips
1 cup (250 mL) crunchy organic peanut butter
1 stick (125 mL) unsalted butter
Pinch of flakey sea salt
10 ounces (280 g) large white marshmallows

Lightly grease a 9-inch (2.5 L) square pan with cooking spray and line with plastic wrap or waxed paper.

In a medium saucepan, bring 1 inch (2.5 cm) of water to a simmer. In a large heatproof bowl, combine the chocolate chips, peanut butter, butter and salt. Place the bowl over the saucepan, ensuring that it does not touch the water, to create a double boiler. Cook, stirring occasionally, until everything is fully melted and smooth. Remove from the heat and let cool for 5 to 6 minutes. Fold in the marshmallows.

Using a rubber spatula, transfer the mixture to the prepared pan and spread it in an even layer. Let chill in the fridge until the chocolate has set, at least 4 hours.

I like to cut all of the squares and freeze half immediately. Store the squares in an airtight container in the fridge for up to 5 days (if they don't get eaten first) or freeze in an airtight container for up to 3 months.

TIP: If you are a texture queen like me, throw in a fistful of puffed grains such as rice, wheat or millet alongside the marshmallows to add a bit of crunch.

WHEN THE RUBBER MEETS THE ROAD

[C] The girls were just over six months old when I strapped them into their car seats, wrestled the dogs into the passenger seat and slid a scratched-up bootleg copy of Bruce Springsteen's *Greatest Hits* into the stereo.

I buckled up. I leaned my head on the steering wheel for what seemed like an hour but was only a few moments. Then I shifted into first gear, and away we went. Two thousand kilometres. Two babies. Two dogs. Three days driving in a fucking blizzard and one in blinding sunshine. But through it all, I felt gratitude that we were in it together, and that everyone's role in the journey was more or less established in advance.

This is where my notes for this essay end and where I freefall into stream of consciousness because I am, at this very moment, sitting in my car using my thumbs to type this as an iPhone note with my now two-and-a-half-year-old daughters in tow.

I've spent the last three days attempting to write about the most challenging and joyful time in my life. The deadline for this book is two weeks away. A few days ago I packed the car with Tetris-like accuracy, jammed the passenger seat with snacks and whisked the girls up to a tiny apartment in Northern Ontario, thinking I could keep them contained and occupied in a new environment with a large TV.

It backfired immediately, and I realized, as I paced the living room on that first night determined to hit a ten-kilometre step count (what I like to call my "sanity threshold"), that I'd contained myself as well. On day two we went to the local big-box store to pick up some emergency pyjamas. Piper had a full-blown meltdown in the stationery aisle.

Later, we tried to go swimming and spent more time getting into and out of our suits than we did in the pool. This morning, determined to just get *outside*, I spent forty-five minutes trying to get everyone (including me) into snow pants. "No!!!" screamed Piper, "I NEED MY BELLY!!!" as she writhed out of her pants before lifting her shirt and placing both palms on her stomach in protest.

And that was it. Trip over. We were booked for another day, but I emptied the fridge, cleared out the dresser and scuttled all the toys into a box. Exhausted. Frustrated.

As I loaded the car, I felt what I always feel while sorting luggage into my trunk. Relief.

I don't have a big car by any stretch of the imagination, and for that I am grateful. I'm able to drive with either hand, assuming I'm not shifting gears, and still reach both car seats. You want a banana? Sure. Bottle's empty? Let me refill it. You want different music? Oh well, mama is enjoying Bonnie Raitt's *Luck of the Draw*.

Sometimes the girls fall asleep. If we're going somewhere, I keep going, but if we're not, I pull over and do what it is I need to do. Sleep. Eat a sandwich. Answer work emails. Write half a book. The car is a safe place. A quiet place. Don't overlook it.

You can be a capable adult and still have limits. You can realize, and be humbled by, just how vastly you underestimated the strength required to be a parent. You can be swallowed whole by anxiety. In those moments, and there have been many, I get in the car. I get in the driver's seat.

Travel Food

Long and short road travel is greatly enhanced by a delicious sandwich. I was introduced to my favourite travel sandwich at Fogo Island Inn in Newfoundland, where you're presented with a brown bag lunch to enjoy on the ferry back to the mainland when you check out. It's very simple but, like all good sandwiches, is more than the sum of its parts and, unlike most sandwiches, has a two- or three-day shelf life.

To make my version of the Fogo travel sandwich, lay out two slices of good dark pumpernickel or rye bread. Spread one slice generously with cream cheese, and on the second add just a skiff of cream cheese. Cover the second piece of bread with sliced white cheddar. Cut the top and bottom off a red bell pepper, use a sharp knife to cut into the pepper and then place the pepper on its side so that you can work your knife (safely) to separate the core from the flesh; you'll end up with a large rectangle of red pepper. Put the red pepper on the cheese and then top it with the other slice of bread. Wrap tightly in waxed paper or a Beeswax Wrap (page 233) and store in the fridge until you're ready to put the pedal to the metal.

A few of my other favourite recipes to prep and pack are:

- Ragamuffins (page 175)
- Freezer Hummus (page 68) with lots of fresh cut veggies and some cubes of cheese
- Spanish Tortilla (page 208) (sometimes I go full Spanish and slice this thinly into a sandwich)
- Antipasto Pasta Salad (page 185)
- Hot Pepper Cornbread (page 219) baked into mini loaves or muffin tins
- 2 AM Cookies (page 158)
- Peanut Butter Marshmallow Squares (page 223) (these are messy but worth it)

HOME ECONOMICS

The part when you're creating a world for your children.

[E] This might strike you as a strange chapter title in a book published in the 2020s by a pair of—I'm going to say it—feminists, but we don't think it's incongruous. It takes skill and a great deal of work to create a happy, restful and, yes, economical home. We are immensely thankful that our foremothers (you don't hear that word much, do you?) successfully fought to expand our educational and professional horizons beyond the home. It is thanks to their efforts, over several generations, that we both have careers that challenge us and are able to contribute to home economics in more ways than one. We are also hugely relieved, especially when we talk to our grandmothers and learn what it was like to raise six children in Sault Ste. Marie, Ontario, on a steel worker's salary in the 1950s and '60s, that household work is no longer the sole domain of women. This progress has been necessary, and there is more to be won. Still, we believe that making a home—a world to come back to and a worthy landscape for childhood—is valuable. We do it with pride, whenever and however we can.

[C] Home economics is about using what you have and using less. It's about rejecting the idea that you need more plastic, more stuff and unitaskers like baby butt wipe warmers. It's getting rid of your microwave (responsibly!) and heating up leftovers in a cast iron pan you got at the thrift store for $2. It's mending clothes and ironing them before you give them to someone who needs them. It's knowing how to balance a cheque book (okay, okay, debit account). It's being the sort of person your grandmother would respect as "thrifty" for myriad reasons, not the least of which is saying, "Hey! I'm going to use that again!" every time your boyfriend tries to throw out that used gallon zip-top bag drying on top of the kitchen faucet.

    It's also about confidence and knowing that you have the resources to handle whatever comes your way. Your kid has a tantrum and the usual strategies don't work? Two words: Play Dough (page 229). Bath time is a screaming, awful, splashy nightmare? Bath Bombs (page 230) to the rescue!

    Finally, it's about doing your best to create more than you consume. Sure, it's easy to buy a cute sheet mask from the pharmacy, but do you have an avocado (A Calming Face Mask, page 242)? We're busy, and you're busy, but this chapter isn't about spending hours rendering lard to make your own soap (I've done it, it's laborious and the recipe is definitely not included). Everything in here is easy to make with ingredients you probably already have in your pantry.

PLAY DOUGH

Makes about 4 cups (1 L), enough to keep a child entertained for at least 20 to 30 minutes

[C] This was a staple in my house growing up. While it's dead easy to make, most people are amazed when I tell them you can make play dough from scratch in less than 10 minutes. I also find it deeply enjoyable and therapeutic to knead when it's still warm, especially after liberally splashing in some lavender or bright citrusy essential oils. If you want to go full hippie mom with this, use natural dyes from vegetables and fruits. Or just raid your pantry for a few drops of food colouring from the last time you made cupcakes.

2 cups (500 mL) all-purpose flour

¾ cup (175 mL) salt

1 tablespoon (15 mL) cream of tartar

2 cups (500 mL) warm water

2 tablespoons (30 mL) cooking oil (any kind! I usually use avocado or coconut)

6 to 8 drops food grade essential oils (optional)

Natural food colouring

In a large saucepan, stir together the flour, salt and cream of tartar. Add the water and oil and cook over medium heat, stirring continuously, until the mixture is thick and comes together to form a ball. Remove the saucepan from the heat and let cool.

When the dough is cool enough to handle, transfer it to a clean, flat surface. Add the essential oils (if using) and knead until the dough is smooth and cool. Divide the dough equally into a number of lumps that matches the number of colours you want to make. For example, if you want to make 3 different colours, divide the dough into 3 lumps. Add a few drops of food colouring to each lump and knead to combine (you may want to place the dough inside a large zip-top bag before kneading in the food colouring to avoid staining your hands).

Bust out the cookie cutters, stamps and that gnocchi board that just sits in your utensil drawer, and let your kids go wild. Store the play dough in an airtight container in the fridge for up to 2 weeks.

BATH BOMBS

Makes 6 large bath bombs

[C] My girls have gone through phases of not wanting to have a bath. That's totally normal and totally frustrating, especially if you're trying to wrestle them through bath time and get a couple hours of, say, writing a cookbook in before you crash as well. This recipe is a good base and, depending on their level of bath time reluctance, you can up the ante by adding dried flowers, food colouring or random tiny prizes that are revealed as the bath bomb dissolves. Good luck!

1 cup (250 mL) baking soda
½ cup (125 mL) cornstarch
½ cup (125 mL) citric acid
½ cup (125 mL) Epsom salt
10 drops food grade essential oil
  (I like lavender)
2 tablespoons (30 mL) virgin
  coconut oil, melted
Natural food colouring (optional)
1 to 2 tablespoons (15 to 30 mL)
  water

In a large bowl, combine the baking soda, cornstarch, citric acid, Epsom salt, essential oil, coconut oil and food colouring, if using. Stir to combine. Add the water 1 tablespoon (15 mL) at a time, kneading with your hands until the texture feels like wet sand.

Tightly pack the mixture into silicone muffin moulds or bath bomb moulds and let dry overnight.

Store the bath bombs in an airtight container at room temperature for up to 6 months.

TIP: Making bath bombs is a great activity to do with your kids. Let them pick scents, colours and fun add-ins like flowers or herbal tea.

BEESWAX WRAPS

Makes about 10 medium wraps

[C] I hate throwing out food, but I also cringe every time I have to wrap up half an onion or two-thirds of a tomato in plastic wrap. A couple of years ago I did some light Googling and started making my own beeswax wraps. They are much easier to make than I thought they would be, and I let my girls pick the fabrics and help me grate the wax blocks.

1 cup (250 mL) beeswax
1 cup (250 mL) pine resin
1 tablespoon (15 mL) virgin
    coconut oil
1 yard (1 metre) natural fibre
    fabric, such as cotton or linen,
    cut into squares
Parchment paper
Ironing board
Iron
Pinking shears

In a medium saucepan, bring 1 inch (2.5 cm) of water to a simmer. In a large heatproof bowl, combine the beeswax, pine resin and coconut oil. Place the bowl over the saucepan, ensuring that it does not touch the water, to create a double boiler. Cook, stirring occasionally, until completely melted. Transfer the mixture to mini loaf pans to set.

To make a wrap, place a large sheet of parchment paper over an ironing board to protect it from the melted wax. On the parchment paper, smooth out a piece of fabric.

Using the largest holes on a box grater, grate a beeswax block and spread about 1 to 2 tablespoons (15 to 30 mL) of beeswax over the piece of fabric in an even layer. Cover with another sheet of parchment paper. Gently iron the parchment paper to melt the wax into the fabric so that it is saturated. Pull off the parchment paper, flip over the fabric and repeat on the second side. It's okay if some of the wax melts off the fabric and onto the parchment paper; you can either save it for the next wrap or chill it and use it at a later date. Hang the waxed fabric over a drying rack to cool and stiffen. Use pinking shears to trim the sides.

Wraps can be cleaned easily using warm (not hot) soapy water and left to dry on a rack. They periodically may need to be rewaxed if they lose their "stick." To do so, simply repeat the steps above with about half the amount of grated beeswax mix.

POTATO STAMPS

Makes 6 potato stamps

[C] Do you really need instructions for making potato stamps? Maybe not. You probably know how to slice a potato in half and cut out a rough heart shape on it. But maybe you've forgotten what a valuable skill this is, and I am here to remind you. At some point, I can guarantee you'll have a screaming toddler on your hands who isn't interested in anything and you'll flip to this page and dig three soft potatoes out of the back of your crisper. In that moment, you'll think, *This book just paid for itself.*

3 potatoes
Washable kids' paint

Cover your work surface with craft paper to protect against possible spills.

Cut the potatoes in half. Using a pencil, draw a shape onto the cut edge of each potato. You can draw a star, triangle, circle, square, heart, large X—or get even more creative. If you want a more refined shape, find some cookie cutters slightly smaller than the circumference of your potato and push them at least ½ inch (1 cm) into the potato. Using a paring knife, cut around each shape so that it is raised from the surface of the potato by at least ½ inch (1 cm).

On your covered work surface, lay out some sheets of paper. Dollop a few colours of paint onto a plate. I like to use primary colours and seize the opportunity to teach basic colour theory. Dip the potato stamps into the paint, making sure to remove any excess paint so that the potato will not slip when stamped. Sit back, relax and let your young Picasso do their thing.

BATH PAINT

Makes 1½ cups (375 mL)

[C] Currently, I have to coax Piper into the bath. While Matilda readily clambers in and starts splishing and splashing, Piper needs additional time and support. Usually, it's a multistep process. First, she grudgingly lets me place her in the tub but refuses to remove the top half of her outfit. After a few more minutes, she might reluctantly sit in the water, but only after I've tied her shirt up around her armpits so it stays out of the water. When the shirt inevitably gets wet, she will then allow me to remove it, at which point she's ready to fully engage with tubtime activities; meanwhile, Matilda has become a raisin. This is a really quick, minimal-waste recipe, and it makes bath time a lot smoother by providing both a point of interest and a happy distraction.

1 cup (250 mL) kid-friendly liquid
    soap (I like Dr. Bronner's)
½ cup (125 mL) cornstarch
Natural food colouring
Food grade essential oils
    (optional)

Place the liquid soap in a medium bowl. Slowly whisk in the cornstarch to form a paste. Continue whisking until no lumps remain.

Divide the paint base among the 6 wells of a standard muffin tin. Add food colouring to create the desired colours. Add essential oils (if using) to reproduce the scents of some of those smelly markers from the early '90s—lemon for yellow, cinnamon for brown, and so on.

Bring the paint into the bath along with some brushes or sponges. If you do not want to use the bath paint immediately—or want to save some for another day—wrap the muffin tin in Beeswax Wrap (page 233) and store it in the fridge for up to 1 week.

FEARS AS FAMILY HEIRLOOMS (OR NOT)

[E] Growing up, my mother was afraid of the things that had killed people around her. Falling through ice on a snowmobile (her best friend's father), burning to death while working at a steel plant (her grandfather) and diving into too-shallow water (her cousin, who became quadriplegic) featured on her list of childhood terrors. So did driving: the cousin she was closest to in age had died at seventeen in a head-on collision with a drunk driver just before Christmas, and her father, having returned from WWII with narcolepsy, sometimes fell asleep at the wheel of the family Mercury.

My mom has written in a journal nearly every day since she was fourteen. The burgundy leatherbound volume that contains my sister's toddlerhood, her pregnancy with me and my first years on the planet in neat ballpoint script now sits at my bedside. She gave it to me when I found out I was pregnant. With it, she issued a warning: "I haven't reread it myself. I hope it's not too shocking."

It is, of course, shocking. My mother wrote for relief, not for a reader. Especially not for the one whose colicky wailing invited more than one dark night of the soul during the bleak postpartum winter of 1988. Her honesty is piercing.

One of the themes she explores is fear. In early motherhood, she strove to confront her fears in order to avoid passing them on to her children. At a rented cottage in July 1988, she wrote of teaching my sister Molly, age two and a half and nervous in water, to feel comfortable in the lake: "We want her to be self-confident, to have the sense of exhilaration that comes with overcoming fears." And then: "I don't want her to be like me."

Although I like to think we are similar to her in some ways, my mom has raised two fearless swimmers. And while she is still uncomfortable with highway driving, she spent nearly two decades ferrying my sister and me to and from school, lessons and friends' houses in a dark green tank we referred to as the "Toyot—" because the "a" had fallen off. Even now, with those duties behind her, she has made a daily practice of white knuckling through Toronto traffic. "If I were to stop, even for a week, I'm not sure I would ever drive again," she told me recently.

Despite my mom's strength of will, the fear of driving still found me. I got my learner's licence at sixteen and then lived overseas for seven years. Upon my return, I failed a road test with flying colours and then did not drive for years. I convinced myself that it is rational to be afraid of driving. Getting into a car is dangerous. Getting into a car with me is, arguably, even more dangerous.

Then I gave birth in a bathtub and briefly felt like Superwoman. High on love and breastfeeding hormones and horrified by the thought that my mom's years of effort helming the Toyot— would be for naught, I decided to become a driver. A good one.

Ezzie was born in January. I booked a road test for May. Encouraged by all of the mothers in my life, including my maternal grandmother, Shirley (an enthusiastic driver into her late eighties who rode shotgun with a narcoleptic for decades, grabbing the wheel when he nodded off), I took lessons with a man named Abdul. Abdul laughed at my fears.

He told me I was great. When I made a wide turn or drifted toward oncoming traffic while checking the wrong blind spot six times for non-existent cyclists, he laughed and told me I just needed to relax, and then I would pass the test, no problem.

When the test day came, I was still breastfeeding every few hours. I nursed Ezzie, handed her to Anthony and drove with Abdul in the passenger seat (on the highway!) to the testing centre. We checked in and waited in Abdul's car.

An hour after my allotted test time, Abdul, aware that I was on a tight feeding schedule, kindly suggested I go into the building and ask how long the delay would be. Then the worst happened: the examiner arrived while I was not in the car. According to the rules of testing centres, this is grounds for instant failure. I ran up to the driver's side door just in time to hear the examiner shout at Abdul, "Well, she should have fed her baby BEFORE the test!"

It was an awkward note to start on, but perhaps the awkwardness worked in my favour: I passed.

That afternoon, my mom took Ezzie and me out for a celebratory lunch, masterfully guiding her long-subdued fear through the unpredictable streets of Toronto, an example to both of us.

About a year later, one of the first objects Ezzie learned to identify was the leased sedan that sits in our driveway and is taken out at least once a week, if not every day.

"Mommy's car," she tells me proudly, pointing at the Toyota with its "a" intact.

FINGER PAINT

Makes about 2 cups (500 mL)

[C] One of the greatest challenges for the modern parent is limiting screen time. Screens are everywhere, and often there are many of them. I fight a losing battle daily to teach my girls that phones are tools and not toys, but it's all undone the minute a babysitter walks through the door and opens up the latest game or starts scrolling through photos and teaching them how to use filters. I know that technology is unavoidable and also terrifically useful (most of this book was written by Emma's and my thumbs, and please don't think that during COVID-19 I didn't rely on it *heavily* to entrance my children while I got meals on the table and endless laundry in the machine), but I do *try*, and having alternative activities and crafts is a must for misdirection. You can make this recipe in less than 5 minutes, plus cooling time, and it is great for individual or group play.

5 tablespoons (75 mL) granulated sugar

½ cup (125 mL) cornstarch

2 cups (500 mL) cold water

Natural food colouring

1 tablespoon (15 mL) glitter (always optional, but also always fun; just take it outside—trust me)

In a medium saucepan, whisk together the sugar and cornstarch. Pour the cold water into the saucepan and whisk until no lumps remain.

Place the saucepan over medium heat and whisk continuously, until the mixture thickens, about 3 to 4 minutes (note: it will thicken more as it cools). Remove the saucepan from the heat.

Divide the mixture among small jars or the 6 wells of a muffin tin. Add food colouring to create the desired colours and glitter, if using. Be sure to put your children in smocks or aprons (or do as I do and remove all their clothes) before giving them paint, brushes or stamps and lots of paper.

Store unused paint, covered, in the fridge for up to 1 week.

A CALMING FACE MASK

Makes 1 face mask

[C] Because you need one, right? Self-care is a challenge. Pausing is a challenge. There are days when, as full of love as you are for your family, you also feel like you have been shot out of a cannon. The thing is, you have to make time for yourself. Not because you deserve it (you do) but because you are the most important person in your children's lives and what you put into yourself, you are actually putting into them. (Read that last line twice; it's important.) It's not about finding time, it's about making time. Read a book, go for a walk, lock yourself in the bathroom once in a while—but just take *care* of yourself.

½ ripe Hass avocado, pitted and peeled

2 tablespoons (30 mL) full-fat plain Greek yogurt (the more probiotic, the better!)

1 tablespoon (15 mL) pure liquid honey

5 drops carrot oil (optional)

In a small bowl, mash the avocado until smooth. Add the yogurt, honey and carrot oil, if using. Stir to combine.

Apply the face mask to clean skin and let sit for 10 to 15 minutes. Rinse with warm water.

ALL-PURPOSE BALM WITH OPTIONS

Makes about 1 cup (250 mL)

[C] This is my go-to recipe for body balm, because it smells great and is easily tweaked to create a range of useful natural cosmetics. I read ingredient lists carefully, including the ones on body care products, especially when it comes to things I'm going to use on my kids. We all spend a lot of time and effort getting our kids to eat right, so it only makes sense to be careful about what we use on their skin as well.

2 tablespoons (30 mL) dried calendula flowers

2 tablespoons (30 mL) dried lavender flowers

½ cup (125 mL) virgin coconut oil

¼ cup (60 mL) shea butter

¼ cup (60 mL) beeswax

1 tablespoon (15 mL) vitamin E oil

In a medium saucepan, bring 2 inches (5 cm) of water to a simmer. In a large heatproof bowl, combine the calendula, lavender, coconut oil, shea butter and beeswax. Place the bowl over the saucepan, ensuring that it does not touch the water, to create a double boiler. Stirring occasionally, let the ingredients melt and allow the herbs to infuse for about 30 minutes. Add the vitamin E oil and stir to combine.

Using a fine-mesh sieve, strain the mixture into a clean jar with a tight-fitting lid. Let cool to room temperature. Cover and let set overnight at room temperature before using.

For Lip Balm
Reduce the amount of coconut oil to ¼ cup (60 mL) and increase the amount of beeswax to ½ cup (125 mL).

For Sun Protector
Add 10 drops carrot seed oil and 4 tablespoons (60 mL) non-nanoparticle zinc oxide powder. Whip with a large whisk as it sets to make it creamy. This doubles as a great barrier cream for diaper rash.

For Beard Oil
Skip the beeswax and use an equal amount of sweet almond oil or jojoba instead. Add 1 teaspoon (5 mL) dried sandal-wood to the bowl with the rest of the ingredients.

TIP: Instead of dried flowers, you can use 10 to 15 drops of food grade essential oils. If you can't find ingredients locally, source them online. Always go for the very best since you're going to slather it all over yourself and your people.

BASIC ALL-PURPOSE CLEANER

Makes 2 cups (500 mL)

[C] This takes a few seconds to whip together and has nothing in the ingredients list that you can't pronounce.

1 cup (250 mL) filtered water
1 cup (250 mL) white vinegar
10 to 15 drops food grade essential
    oil of choice (I like lemongrass)

Using a funnel, pour the water and vinegar into a clean spray bottle. Add the essential oil, put on the lid and shake vigorously.

Spray the cleaner onto counters, walls, and so on and wipe off with a clean, damp cloth.

THE EXCHANGE

[C] I was twenty-one years old the first time my grandmother told me she loved me. We were leaving a holiday dinner, and she was trying to put her hand through a buttonhole in her coat. Earlier, she'd tried to eat a scoop of chocolate gelato with those same gnarled but manicured fingers. As I was helping her, guiding her bird-like arm gently into the sleeve, she looked at me, her eyes cleared and she said with force, "I love you, Christine." And then again, whimpering, "I really love you."

When her diagnosis came in, I was a teenager. I didn't know what Alzheimer's was. I didn't know how much it would take from us. I didn't know how much it would give. It's a gut punch of a disease, but the fist that punches lingers. It tears everything out, showing it to you as it's tossed away, until there is nothing left but emptiness.

My grandmother never got to see me grow up. She only knew me as the person with the problem, never as the person with the solution. And still, she loved me, quietly and with composure, until the disease took away her inhibitions and her Catholic sensibilities and she could be honest with me. Then she was gone, and all I had left was her pencil box and a handwritten book of recipes.

That composure, that inability to talk about feelings—it's in me, too. As I smoothed Grandma's coat over her shoulders that night, and then gripped her hand to help her down the stairs, I could only mumble something back that wasn't equal to what she had given me.

For me, words are hard. A cake is easy. In the extremes of happiness or grief, I am always worried about saying the wrong thing, of not being able to express myself correctly. But a casserole never says the wrong thing. A loaf of bread can fill a silence in the exact right way.

Today, Piper held up a fat fistful of crackers. Spewing Wheat Thin crumbs onto my leg, she announced, "For you, Mama!" and I thought, *Oh, you are so my child*. I took a nibble, enjoying the offering and the moment, and then apropos of nothing, she said to me, "I love you, Mama. I really love you."

It's a beautiful thing, the way food and love intertwine. How one picks up where the other leaves off. When you are young, it's an obvious and immediate transaction. When you are older, it's a gift to be able to conjure someone who has left you to the table, with a pasta salad or a platter of ginger cake, and it's as if they are right there, eyes twinkling, dry martini clinking.

I cook for my kids because I love them. That's the best piece of me I can give. The thought, the time, the love. Sometimes they eat it, sometimes they whip it at the wall and declare it "Gross!" And in those moments, I'm getting better with my words. I love you, Piper. I love you, Matilda. I love you, Grandma. I made this for you.

BUILDING BLOCKS

Stocks, sauces, spreads and one dough.

PIZZA DOUGH

Makes enough dough for 2 standard pizzas

[C] Well, yes, it's a pizza dough recipe, but pizza dough is to me what a large cardboard box is to my children. The options are endless. It's not a pizza, it's a flatbread. Fold it over and it's a calzone. Tear some holes in it and it's a fougasse! Roll it into buns. Tie it into garlic knots. Bake it. Fry it. Grill it. Anything is possible, but you do have to make the dough first.

1½ cups (375 mL) all-purpose flour, more for kneading

½ cup (125 mL) whole wheat flour

1 tablespoon (15 mL) pure liquid honey or sugar

1 cup (250 mL) lukewarm water

1 tablespoon (15 mL) yeast

1 teaspoon (5 mL) anise or fennel seed (optional)

2 tablespoons (30 mL) extra-virgin olive oil, more for greasing

1 teaspoon (5 mL) salt

In a small bowl, stir together the all-purpose and whole wheat flours.

In a large bowl, stir together the honey and water, until the honey is dissolved. Sprinkle in the yeast and let sit for 10 minutes, until bubbly. Using a wooden spoon, stir in the flour mixture, anise (if using), oil and salt. Continue stirring until the mixture comes together in a kneadable ball of dough.

Lightly flour a large clean surface such as a cutting board or countertop, then tip the dough out onto the surface. With lightly floured hands, knead the dough for about 10 minutes, until it is no longer tacky.

TIP: I find kneading to be very calming and meditative, and sometimes I give my girls a piece of dough to work with when I'm kneading by hand; they enjoy working alongside me and "helping," and it helps me enjoy the process even more. If you want to make your dough in a stand mixer, that's fine, too—just reduce the "kneading time" by about half.

Lightly grease a medium bowl with olive oil. Lightly grease the dough ball and place it in the bowl. Cover and let rest in a warm (but not hot) place to rise, until it has doubled in size, about 40 minutes. Punch down the dough.

If you are hoping to eat right away, make Greens and Cheese Grandma Slice (page 130) or Fattoush with a Side of Flatbread (142), or roll the dough into the preferred shape and bake, grill, fry, etc., as desired. If you want to use the dough later, oil it generously with more olive oil, place it in a bowl, cover it with a clean dish towel and store it in the fridge for up to 12 hours. Just be sure to let it come to room temperature before you try to use it. You can also divide the dough and freeze it in zip-top bags for up to 3 months. To use from frozen, remove the dough from the bag, oil it with olive oil and let it come to room temperature before baking as usual.

QUICK PICKLED VEGETABLES

Makes about 2 cups (500 mL) pickling liquid, or enough for 2 (16-ounce/500 mL) mason jars

[C] Although I appreciate the effort and patience it takes to ferment pickled vegetables the old-fashioned way, I don't have the time or countertop real estate for that. Making pickled vegetables with this liquid is so fast, I like to call them "quickles." They are more or less done by the time the brine cools.

PICKLING LIQUID

2 cups (500 mL) rice wine vinegar

¼ cup (60 mL) granulated sugar
   or sweetener of choice

FOR PICKLING

4 cups (1 L) chopped or sliced
   vegetables of choice (see Tip)

To make the pickling liquid, in a medium saucepan over high heat, whisk together the vinegar and sugar. Bring to a boil. Remove the brine from the heat.

To pickle the vegetables, divide the vegetables evenly between 2 (16-ounce/500 mL) mason jars with tight-fitting lids. Pour the pickling liquid over the prepared vegetables, dividing it evenly between the jars. Let cool to room temperature.

Store the pickles in the jars, with the lid tightly fastened, in the fridge for up to 3 months. Be sure to use a clean utensil to get them out of the jar.

TIP: Pickled red onions are a fridge staple in my house. They are bright and colourful, so the girls like eating them. They really jazz up a chicken sandwich and can easily be tossed into a salad. Other vegetables that are great for pickling are carrots, turnips, beets and celery.

VEGETABLE STOCK

Makes about 12 cups (3 L)

[C] In most recipes where we call for water (baking aside!), you can use stock instead for more flavour and nutrition. I love using up whatever is looking tired in the crisper, such as that half a head of celery from two weeks ago, as well as trimmings from onions, carrots and leek tops. Rutabaga is a delicious vegetable and adds both an earthiness and a sweetness to this stock, but be sure to remove the waxy coating on it, if there is one, before adding it to your stock.

¼ cup (60 mL) olive oil

2 large yellow onions, quartered

1 large fennel bulb, quartered

1 medium rutabaga, quartered

2 medium zucchinis, cut into
   2-inch (5 cm) chunks

2 large carrots, cut into 2-inch
   (5 cm) chunks

3 stalks celery, cut into 2-inch
   (5 cm) chunks

Cold water to cover (about
   1 gallon/4 L)

In a large stockpot, heat the olive oil over medium-high heat. Add the vegetables and decrease the heat to medium so that they sweat but do not brown. Cook for about 7 to 10 minutes, stirring frequently.

Cover the vegetables with the cold water, making sure that everything is submerged. Increase the heat to medium-high. Bring to a boil. Reduce the heat to low and let simmer and bubble away for 1 hour.

Using a fine-mesh sieve, strain the solids out of the stock. Return the pot to the stove and continue to simmer until the stock is reduced by half.

Store the stock in an airtight container in the fridge for up to 1 week or freeze in zip-top bags for up to 3 months.

TIP: You can put just about anything in vegetable stock, but avoid things like pumpkin, potato or other starchy vegetables that will make it cloudy.

CHICKEN STOCK

Makes about 12 cups (3 L)

[C] When I needed stock for a recipe at culinary school, they'd send me to the fridge with a ladle. When I worked in France, they'd send me to the fridge with a knife. There are definitely two schools of thought on how thick you want this stock to be, but in either case I like to keep it really neutral (no salt, garlic or heavy flavours) so that if I choose to reduce it, the flavours don't become overpowering.

4 bone-in chicken breasts
2 large onions, quartered
2 large carrots, cut into 2-inch
 (5 cm) chunks
3 stalks celery, cut into 2-inch
 (5 cm) chunks
Cold water to cover (about
 1 gallon/4 L)

Place the chicken and vegetables in a large stockpot. Cover with the cold water, making sure that everything is submerged. Place over medium-high heat and bring to a boil. Reduce the heat to low and let simmer for about 20 minutes, until the chicken is cooked through. Remove the chicken and set aside. Once the chicken is cool enough to handle, pick all of the meat from the bones and reserve for another use. Return the bones to the pot (it is fine if some meat remains attached; this will only add flavour). Continue to simmer, uncovered, for 40 minutes.

Using a fine-mesh sieve, strain the solids out of the stock.

Store the stock in an airtight container in the fridge for up to 1 week or freeze in zip-top bags for up to 3 months. Another option for freezing the stock is to continue simmering, uncovered, until it is reduced by half. This will yield a concentrated stock. Freeze it in ice cube trays before transferring the cubes to zip-top bags or a container to store for up to 3 months. You can easily slip the cubes of stock into a soup or stew to add more flavour. (My mom also does this with half-finished bottles of wine, which can be used to add flavour as well.)

TIP: If you're looking to add more body to your stock without reducing it, ask your butcher if they have chicken feet for sale. Put them in the saucepan along with the chicken and they will add natural gelatin and collagen, which thickens the stock and is great for your skin and nails.

ROASTED APPLESAUCE

Makes 2 to 3 cups (500 to 750 mL)

[C] It's always handy to have a jar of applesauce in the fridge. Because the apples are roasted, they blend easily and the sauce has a caramelized sweetness to it. Apple skins have natural pectin, so the sauce gets nice and thick and doesn't have that grainy, watery texture you get when you simply boil apples and mash them. While this recipe is certainly kid-friendly, it's also multi-use. Dip other fruit in it, spread it on toast and sprinkle with cinnamon, serve alongside pierogies or pork roast or use it in lieu of other sweeteners in baked goods, smoothies, soups—you name it!

4 to 5 large apples such as Fuji, Pink Lady or Honeycrisp

Preheat the oven to 400°F (200°C). Spray a large baking sheet with cooking spray.

Cut the apples in half and use a melon baller (if you happen to have one, otherwise a paring knife will do) to remove the cores. Use a paring knife to trim out any remaining stem. Place the apples, cut side down, on the prepared baking sheet, ensuring that they do not touch each other or they will steam instead of roast. If your apples are really large, you may need 2 baking sheets.

Roast the apples for about 15 minutes, until they are soft and have released some of their juices. Remove from the oven and let cool for 5 minutes.

Place the apples and any juice from the baking sheets in a high-speed blender and blend until smooth.

Store the applesauce in an airtight jar or container in the fridge for up to 1 week.

TIP: Purchasing good-quality food can really make a dent in your budget. Roasting any aging fruit from your fruit bowl (bruised peaches, shrivelled plums, softer-than-ideal pears, and so on) and blending them along with the apples is a great way to help cut down on food waste.

CINNAMON PECAN BUTTER

Makes about ⅔ cup (150 mL)

[E] If your dreams are made of nut butter, as mine are, then you'll eat this with a spoon. And spread it on toasted challah with an extra sprinkle of cinnamon. And dip apples in it, stuff dates with it, drizzle it on Greek yogurt with a handful of Really Crunchy Granola (page 19), add a dollop to your oatmeal and use it in a Green Ginger Smoothie (page 163).

2 cups (500 mL) raw pecan halves
Pinch of salt
½ teaspoon (2 mL) ground
　cinnamon

Preheat the oven to 350°F (180°C). Line a rimmed baking sheet with a Silpat or parchment paper.

Spread the pecans in an even layer on the prepared baking sheet. Toss with salt and cinnamon. Toast for 10 to 15 minutes, or until delicious-smelling and deep brown.

Place the pecans in the bowl of a food processor (it's okay if they're still warm—it will only make the butter more delicious) and blend on high speed, until they go from crumbly to smooth and buttery, about 1 minute. Scrape down the sides of the bowl with a spatula. Blend again until smooth.

Store in an airtight jar in the fridge for 2 to 3 weeks.

RASPBERRY CHIA JAM

Makes about 2 cups (500 mL)

[C] Dead simple to make and no sugar required. You can sweeten with a drizzle of pure liquid honey or pure maple syrup, but if you're using good-quality fruit, I find it's sweet enough. This jam is great served with a slice of toast and some Cinnamon Pecan Butter (page 257), and it's a great topper for Cold Fruits Smoothie Bowl (page 23), Sour Cream Scones (page 97), Golden Milk Chia Pudding (page 107) or Pancakes for the People (page 166).

1 pound (450 g) frozen raspberries
2 tablespoons (30 mL) chia seeds
Pure liquid honey or pure maple
　syrup, to taste (optional)

In a small bowl, use a fork to smash together the frozen raspberries and chia seeds. Let thaw at room temperature for 2 hours. Stir until the mixture has a loose jam consistency. Stir in the honey, if using.

Store in an airtight container in the fridge for up to 1 week.

MILDRED'S YOGURT SAUCE

Makes about 1 cup (250 mL)

[C] My grandmother Mildred was the sort of woman who set the table the day before she hosted a dinner party. She had two wedding rings. One, which was her actual wedding ring, and another, a simple gold band, which she put on when she removed her real ring in order to do dishes or a bit of gardening. My other grandmother, Marge, would go out of her way to buy Frosted Flakes, Corn Pops and the like when we visited, but Mildred didn't budge from her (extremely Catholic) breakfast of All-Bran, conceding only a little to allow us 1 tablespoon (15 mL) of golden raisins on top if we asked nicely. These days, I wear her utility wedding ring on my right hand, and I think of her often, especially when I make this sauce, which she served regularly with fresh fruit or a bit of cake in lieu of something more decadent like ice cream or whipped cream.

1 cup (250 mL) full-fat plain Greek yogurt
Zest and juice of 1 navel orange
1 teaspoon (5 mL) pure vanilla extract

In a small bowl, whisk everything together, until combined. If you think of it, you can make this sauce the night before you want to serve it (perhaps while you are setting the table for your guests the next day) and the flavours will be even better.

Serve with fresh fruit or as a sauce for Polenta Peach Cake (page 220).

Store the sauce in an airtight container in the fridge for up to 1 week.

TIP: Put this sauce out with a platter of cut-up fruits as a dip for kids.

LEMON CURD

Makes about 3 cups (750 mL)

[C] Don't let the word "curd" fool you; this recipe tastes better than it sounds, and it's incredibly versatile. Put it on Pancakes for the People (page 166), thick-spread it on toast, add a dollop to a bowl of ice cream or schmear it on Sour Cream Scones (page 97), should you so be inspired.

2 cups (500 mL) granulated sugar

Juice of 3 lemons

4 whole eggs, beaten

4 egg yolks, beaten

1 stick cold unsalted butter, cut into cubes

In a medium saucepan, bring 2 inches (5 cm) of water to a simmer. In a large heatproof bowl, whisk together the sugar, lemon juice, eggs and egg yolks, until combined. Place the bowl over the saucepan, ensuring that it does not touch the water, to create a double boiler. You want the steam to heat the bowl, but you don't want the mixture to be over direct heat or you will scramble the eggs. Using a heatproof spatula, stir continuously for 7 to 10 minutes, until the mixture becomes thick and glossy.

Carefully remove the bowl from the heat (there's a lot of hot steam under there) and, using a fine-mesh sieve, strain the curd into a medium bowl. Drop in the butter, 1 cube at a time, stirring to incorporate it fully before adding the next cube.

Transfer the lemon curd to an airtight container and let set in the fridge for 2 hours. Store in an airtight container in the fridge for up to 2 weeks.

AIOLI

Makes about 1½ cups (375 mL)

[C] Emma's deep and abiding hatred of mayonnaise aside, I think a good aioli can really elevate a dish. This recipe is super adaptable. Add a squirt of Sriracha sauce and you'll have spicy mayo, or you can chop up some pickles and capers to throw in and make tartar sauce. It's a snap to make; just don't rush it when you add the oil, or the dressing will split.

1 to 2 cloves garlic, chopped

1 egg

1 egg yolk

1 tablespoon (15 mL) Dijon
    mustard

Zest and juice of 1 lemon

½ cup (125 mL) neutral oil, such as
    canola or grapeseed

½ cup (125 mL) extra-virgin
    olive oil

Salt and pepper

In a high-speed blender, pulse the garlic, egg, egg yolk, mustard and lemon zest and juice until smooth.

With the blender running on low, slowly stream in the neutral oil and then the olive oil. Continue blending, until fully incorporated. Season with salt and pepper, to taste, and pulse to combine. If the aioli has become thicker than you would like, drizzle in 1 tablespoon (15 mL) water or lemon juice and pulse, until combined.

Using a rubber spatula, transfer the aioli to an airtight container and store in the fridge for up to 1 week.

TZATZIKI

Makes about 2½ cups (625 mL)

[C] Hands down, this is my favourite condiment for slathering onto warm flatbread and loading with crunchy vegetables. I use Skyr or Greek yogurt so that it has extra protein and is extra thick, and even though I love a good spread, this recipe is also great for dunking and dipping.

1 seedless cucumber, grated
Pinch of salt
2 cups (500 mL) full-fat plain Greek or Skyr yogurt
2 cloves garlic, smashed and minced
1 to 2 tablespoons (15 to 30 mL) white vinegar
1 to 2 tablespoons (15 to 30 mL) chopped fresh dill
Extra-virgin olive oil, for garnish

In a colander or fine-mesh sieve, toss the cucumber with the salt and let drain for 15 to 20 minutes. Press down on the cucumber to squeeze out as much liquid as possible.

In a small bowl, stir together the yogurt, garlic, vinegar and dill. Stir in the cucumber. Drizzle with olive oil before serving.

Store the tzatziki in an airtight container in the fridge for up to 1 week.

TIP: A handful of chopped mint is a nice addition to this recipe. Stir it in with the cucumber.

PESTO CHANGE-O

Makes about 1 cup (250 mL)

[C] Almost anything is enhanced by a schmear of pesto. Brush it on grilled fish; spread it on a chicken, apple, Gruyère and butter lettuce sandwich; toss it with some pasta or dollop it onto a wedge of quiche. Pine nuts are the typical nut used in pesto, but after years of dealing with nut allergies in my restaurants, I always reach for seeds when making this recipe. In addition, while I'm all for serving the world's most expensive nut as a feature item, anytime I'm blending something beyond recognition, I tend to opt for a cheaper substitute that tastes just as good.

2 cloves garlic, roughly chopped

2 tablespoons (30 mL) sunflower or pumpkin seeds

Zest and juice of 1 lemon

1 teaspoon (5 mL) salt

1 cup (250 mL) lightly packed fresh basil

1 cup (250 mL) lightly packed kale or arugula

½ cup (125 mL) extra-virgin olive oil

¼ cup (60 mL) grated Pecorino Romano cheese

In a high-speed blender, combine the garlic, sunflower seeds, lemon zest and juice and salt. Pulse until smooth. Unplug the blender. Add the basil and kale and pack them down into the bottom of the blender jar. Plug the blender back in and blend on high. If your blender has a tamper stick, use it to press down the herbs and help them blend. With the blender running, slowly stream in the olive oil and blend until smooth. Sprinkle in the Pecorino and pulse a couple of times to combine.

Transfer the pesto to an airtight container and store in the fridge for up to 1 month or freeze indefinitely.

LEMON VINAIGRETTE

Makes about 1 cup (250 mL)

[C] This is my favourite dressing for a simple arugula salad with a couple of slices of hard pear and a shaving or two of Pecorino Romano cheese. Because of the rice wine vinegar, this vinaigrette leans toward sweet on the spectrum, but the lemon juice gives it sharpness and wakes up whatever you're drizzling it over.

3 tablespoons (45 mL) fresh lemon juice

3 tablespoons (45 mL) rice wine vinegar

1 tablespoon (15 mL) pure liquid honey

1 tablespoon (15 mL) Dijon mustard

⅔ cup (150 mL) canola oil or oil of choice

In a medium bowl, whisk together the lemon juice, vinegar, honey and mustard. Slowly drizzle in the canola oil, whisking all the while, until fully incorporated.

Use immediately or store in an airtight container in the fridge for up to 2 weeks. If the dressing separates, simply shake the container vigorously before use to combine.

TIP: Canola gets a bad rap, but it's a great oil if sourced and processed properly. I use a local, cold-pressed, organic canola oil from Pristine Gourmet; in addition to having a vibrant yellow colour and clean flavour, it's great for frying, finishing vegetables, fish and meats, and I use it in my homemade body care products because I've seen where it's grown and pressed. If you can't find a good source for local canola oil, sunflower and grapeseed oil are also great options.

BALSAMIC VINAIGRETTE

Makes about 1 cup (250 mL)

[C] Perfect with a hearty mix of baby greens, a few chunks of good blue cheese and a smattering of toasted pecans. However, this dressing is only as good as the balsamic vinegar you buy. If you only have cheap balsamic, you can fake it till you make it by adding 1 tablespoon (15 mL) port per cup of balsamic. If you're thinking, *Aha! I better go buy some port*, skip that and just buy some good-quality balsamic vinegar from Modena in a dark bottle and keep it in a cupboard away from the light.

¼ cup (60 mL) balsamic vinegar

1 tablespoon (15 mL) pure maple
    syrup (optional)

1 tablespoon (15 mL) Dijon
    mustard

½ small shallot, minced

¾ cup (175 mL) extra-virgin
    olive oil

Salt and pepper

In a medium bowl, whisk together the vinegar, maple syrup (if using), mustard and shallot. Whisking continuously, slowly drizzle in the olive oil, until fully combined. Add salt and pepper, to taste.

Use immediately or store in an airtight container in the fridge for up to 2 weeks. If the dressing separates, simply shake the container vigorously before use to combine.

TIP: If you're whisking and the bowl keeps rattling around in a circle, briefly run a dish towel under water to dampen it. Twist it into a snake (like you're about to get into a wet towel fight in a football change room) and turn it into a circle. Set it on your work surface with the bowl on top so that the bowl is resting on the towel, not on the work surface. Continue whisking.

GREEN RANCH

Makes just over 1 cup (250 mL)

[C] Ranch is herbaceous and cooling, adds a creaminess to crisp lettuces and vegetables or acts as a counterpoint to charred and flavourful meats. For this recipe, you can use aioli or prepared mayonnaise, but you can also sub in an equal amount of full-fat plain Greek yogurt or Skyr for a bit more protein and tang.

1 tablespoon (15 mL) chopped fresh dill
1 tablespoon (15 mL) chopped fresh parsley
1 green onion, ends trimmed and chopped
¾ cup (175 ml) Aioli (page 260) or prepared
   mayonnaise

1 tablespoon (15 mL) lemon juice
½ teaspoon (2 mL) garlic powder
½ teaspoon (2 mL) onion powder
2 tablespoons (30 mL) water
Salt and pepper, to taste

Place everything in a high-speed blender and purée until smooth.

Use immediately or store in an airtight container in the fridge for up to 1 week.

LIME CREMA

Makes about 1 cup (250 mL)

[C] Serving dressings and sauces that aren't ketchup to kids is important. First, it's a great way to build flavour or add creaminess, and second, small mouths don't produce as much saliva as big ones. So, adding moisture to food to help children chew, enjoy and digest food more easily. This is a basic taco sauce recipe, and you can plop it on tacos, quesadillas, burritos or just leftovers with a bit of rice and some hot sauce for a burrito bowl–type experience.

1 cup (250 mL) full-fat sour cream
   or crème fraîche
¼ cup (60 mL) fresh cilantro
   leaves and stems, chopped
Zest and juice of 1 lime
1 tablespoon (15 mL) caper juice

Place everything in a high-speed blender and purée until smooth.

Use immediately or store in an airtight container in the fridge for up to 1 week.

TIP: Like all soft herbs (parsley, tarragon, and so on), most of the flavour in cilantro is in the stem. So, if you are going to be chopping or puréeing cilantro, use everything but the root to minimize food waste and maximize flavour.

ACKNOWLEDGEMENTS

[E] I would like to thank my teachers: Esmé Beatrice for showing me, patiently, how to be her mom and for being her strong, sweet self. Anthony Green, my partner in all things, for his steadying perspective during dark nights (and in the shockingly early morning, too). Colleen Flood for forming my foundational understanding of motherhood, with her bottomless depths of ingenuity, empathy and love—and for her encouragement and edits. Denyse Green for remembering, noticing and regularly providing support I didn't know I needed—and for treating me as a daughter. Sophie Green for setting the kindest, most generous example of early motherhood I can imagine. Doug Knight for listening carefully and for making the kitchen seem like a place where quiet wonders can occur. Molly Knight for showing her weird little sister what courage looks like and for being one of Ezzie's favourite and most relied-upon people. Shelley Ambrose for treating all of us like interesting, accountable grown-ups well before that was true. Shirley Daynard for expanding my idea of what's possible. Don Green for being one of the biggest-hearted dads and grandfathers I've ever known and for his calming gestures, words and presence. Matt Kliegman for sharing his wisdom, Zen and perfectly plated breakfasts. Deeva Green and Lee Reitelman for always getting it, no matter what *it* is, and for their passion in the kitchen. Monica Ainley de La Villardière for helping me see what's important. My fairy godmother Gail White for her minestrone and for her brilliant thesis, which started me thinking. My partner Hana James for her generosity with everything, including some Greenhouse recipes. Houley Bah and Christina Gordon for trusting me and helping me trust myself. Geraldine Dempsey for giving us a community when we so desperately needed one. Dawn Payne for loving us like her own. Marly Julian and Gina Dulay for mothering us. Christine, my favourite chef, for putting her whole heart and brain into this labour of love. Alyssa Wodabek, Chris Sue-Chu (and Emily Macri!), Lindsay Guscott and Emily Howes for making the process fun and the photos edible. Laura Dosky for her kind way of wielding both an excellent ear and a fine-tooth comb. Rick Broadhead, Andrea Magyar and the team at Penguin Random House for making it real. All the moms and mother figures in the world for doing a stellar job of holding it down.

[C] A tremendous thank you to Janice and Greg for the seventeen-year parenting intensive and for your continued support even from afar. Another thank you to the many people who have helped to raise me into and through adulthood: Allan and Celia, Meg and Rob, Chris and Nancy, Denis and Susan, Mark and Beth, Rolf and Cindy, Kath and Jim, Pat and Mark.

Denise, I can never repay the wisdom and kindness you imparted to me on those late nights in the dishpit or on those sweaty walks carrying the laundry. Suzanne, thank you for scooping me off the floor on more than one occasion and for being the person I talk to when I'm in the kind of trouble I need an adult for. To my brothers, thanks for the power tools. To my sister, Jordan, thanks for being one. Alan, Devon, Art and Nat, thank you for letting me be a mother—none of this would be possible if I didn't have your support. Shahir, where would I be without you in my corner? René, never underestimate how much you shaped me as a chef. Thank you to Kris, Hassel, Kasia, Sherry, Misha, Bethany, Rossy, Wawa and Char for your unwavering and fierce support; it has meant the world to us. Zach and Rosa, you helped me build a home, literally. Bas, thank you for always picking up when I call. Hannah, you saved me. Ganz gut. Brilynn, thank you for the late-night chats and early-morning exits. I wouldn't want to be quarantined with anyone else. Andrew, I love you for always being the good kind of distraction.

Samy and Ruth, Dorothy and Yves, Peg and Bill thank you for being excellent grandparents.

To the many people I have had the pleasure of working with over the years, thank you—and I'm sorry if I was wound too tight. I'm working on it.

Bruce Springsteen, if you've read this far, thanks for that. If not, I appreciate everything you've done to get me through the last few years. You've been a huge help.

Emma, thank you for collaborating with me and being patient with my quirks. Rick, Andrea and Laura, for believing in this project and in us. Alyssa, Chris, Lindsay, Emily and Emily, thanks for being a crack team and for eating our leftovers instead of ordering in.

Marge and Ivan, Mildred and Jim—I think of you every day, and I wish you could see that I have ended up with not just your work ethic but also your recipes. Matilda and Piper, you are my whole world. Thank you for choosing me.

INDEX